RETHINKING
PROJECT
MANAGEMENT

Transforming Project Delivery
with Generative AI

Sheldon St. Clair PhD

Copyright © 2024 Sheldon St. Clair

All rights reserved.

DEDICATION

To all the project managers who strive for excellence every day.

May this book help you use Generative AI to make your jobs easier, work more efficiently, and complete great projects.

CONTENTS

	Acknowledgments	i
	Why I Wrote This Book: A Personal Reflection	1
	Introduction: Embracing AI in Project Management	5
1.	Disrupting Project Management Norms	9
	Challenge traditional project management notions.	9
	What is Text-Based Generative AI Chatbots?	14
	Present problems with current project workflows	19
	Exploring the need for text-based generative AI chatbots	22
2.	Gaining Insights with Text-Based Generative AI Chatbots	29
	Understanding AI Capabilities in Project Management	29
	Case Studies: AI Chatbots Transforming Projects	34
	Insights into Future Project Management Trends	39
	Ethical Considerations and the Human Touch in AI Integration	43
3.	The PMAI Method in Action	49
	Define and Plan with AI (D&P)	50
	Summarize and Focus using AI (S&F)	53
	Analyze and Insight through AI (A&I)	56
	Risk and Strategy with AI Support (R&S)	60
	Delegate and Track by AI (D&T)	64

SHELDON ST. CLAIR

Report and communicate via AI (R&C)	68
Knowledge and Standards Centralization (K&S)	72
Allocate and Optimize Resources (A&O)	75
Train and Onboard with AI Assistance (T&O)	79
Generate and Refine project content (G&R)	83

4. Overcoming Objections to AI Adoption — **89**

Addressing Doubts About AI Reliability	89
Overcoming Resistance to AI in Project Management	90
AI Won't Replace Human Project Managers	92
Debunking Myths About AI Complexity and Cost	93
Alleviating Fears About AI Errors and Biases	95
Balancing Human-AI Collaboration Challenges	97
Starting Small: Practical First Steps with AI	99
Building Self-Belief and Evaluating ROI	100
When is the Right Time to Adopt AI?	102
Managing Time and Budget for AI Implementation	104

5. Implementing the PMAI Method — **107**

Encouraging Engagement with AI Chatbots	108
Next Steps to Adopt the PMAI Method	109
Becoming a Pioneer in AI-Driven Project Management	110
Embracing the Future with the PMAI Method	111
Conclusions: The Future Is AI	**113**

RETHINK PROJECT MANAGEMENT

Next Steps   117

About The Author   119

ACKNOWLEDGMENTS

I am deeply grateful to my family, friends, colleagues, and mentors who supported me throughout this journey. Thank you to the project management professionals who shared their insights and experiences, which enriched this book's content. Your wisdom and encouragement made this achievement possible.

WHY I WROTE THIS BOOK: A PERSONAL REFLECTION

Over my many years working as a project manager in the fast-paced IT industry, I've experienced countless challenges and obstacles. From wrestling with rapidly evolving technologies to managing remote teams across multiple time zones, the demands of this field can often feel overwhelming.

Yet, amidst the complexities, I've also witnessed the incredible potential for project managers to drive innovation, enhance efficiency, and deliver solutions that transform businesses and delight customers. This duality of difficulties and opportunities is what initially inspired me to write this book.

As project managers, we stand at the intersection of people, processes, and technology. On one hand, we must navigate the intricacies of cutting-edge systems, stringent security protocols, and strict compliance requirements. On the other, we must cultivate strong team dynamics, manage stakeholder expectations, and inspire our colleagues to embrace change.

Over the years, I've seen far too many talented project managers struggle under the weight of these competing demands. They become bogged down by administrative tasks, drowning in a deluge of emails, meetings, and documentation. This robs them of the time and energy needed to truly excel in their strategic roles as leaders and problem-solvers.

It was witnessing this paradox that motivated me to explore how modern technologies, particularly advancements in artificial intelligence (AI), could alleviate some of these burdens. I wanted to find a way for project managers to offload the tedious, repetitive aspects of their work to intelligent systems, freeing them to focus on the high-level thinking, decision-making, and interpersonal elements that drive project success.

Through extensive research and experimentation, I discovered the game-changing potential of generative AI chatbots tailored explicitly for project management. These conversational AI assistants can streamline everything from project planning and risk assessment to task delegation and status reporting. Rather than being replaced by AI, project managers can utilize it as a force multiplier, amplifying their abilities and impact.

This realization was transformative for me, both professionally and personally. I saw an opportunity to share these insights with my colleagues and peers in the project management community. By equipping them with the knowledge and tools to harness the power of AI, I could empower them to overcome the obstacles that have long hindered their journey towards achieving their desired "prizes" – be it successful project delivery, career advancement, recognition as industry leaders, or personal fulfillment.

With this vision in mind, I embarked on a mission to create a comprehensive guidebook that would demystify AI integration for project managers. This book aims to provide a clear roadmap for harnessing these cutting-edge technologies, complete with practical strategies, real-world examples, and a framework for seamless implementation.

Ultimately, my goal is to equip my fellow project managers with the knowledge and tools they need to thrive in the current landscape while future-proofing their skillsets for the rapidly evolving world of tomorrow. By leveraging AI as a force multiplier, we can collectively elevate our profession, drive innovation, and ensure that project management remains a catalyst for organizational success in the digital age.

4

INTRODUCTION: EMBRACING AI IN PROJECT MANAGEMENT

The world of project management is evolving rapidly, and those who embrace new technologies like artificial intelligence (AI) will be the ones leading the charge. This book is your guide to harnessing the power of AI chatbots to revolutionize how you plan, execute, and deliver projects successfully.

By the end of this book, you'll understand the immense potential of AI integration in project management. You'll gain practical strategies to implement AI chatbots as virtual assistants, automate tedious tasks, and make data-driven decisions with ease. Whether you're a seasoned project manager or just starting, this book will equip you with the tools to thrive in the AI-driven future.

THE EMERGING ROLE OF AI CHATBOTS

Imagine having an ever-present digital assistant by your side, one that can understand and communicate just like a human. This is the reality that AI chatbots are bringing to project management.

AI chatbots are computer programs that use natural language processing to comprehend human language and respond accordingly. They can analyze data, identify patterns, and provide insights to support decision-making. And in project management, their applications are endless.

AI chatbots can assist with everything from creating schedules and tracking progress to summarizing meeting notes and generating reports. They can identify potential risks, suggest mitigation plans, and optimize resource allocation. By automating repetitive tasks, these virtual assistants free up your time to focus on the strategic aspects of project delivery.

PRESENT PROBLEMS AND AI CHATBOT SOLUTIONS

While project management methodologies have evolved, several persistent challenges continue to hinder success. AI chatbots offer innovative solutions to these longstanding problems:

1. **Scope creep and schedule delays:** AI chatbots can continuously monitor project scope, timelines, and dependencies, flagging potential deviations and recommending corrective actions.
2. **Ineffective communication:** With their natural language abilities, AI chatbots can streamline communication among team members, stakeholders, and clients, ensuring everyone stays informed and aligned.
3. **Suboptimal resource utilization:** By analyzing historical data and current project needs, AI chatbots can optimize resource allocation, avoiding under- or over-utilization.
4. **Lack of real-time insights:** AI chatbots can integrate with

various data sources, providing up-to-the-minute status updates, risk assessments, and actionable insights.

5. **Repetitive administrative tasks:** From scheduling meetings to generating routine reports, AI chatbots can automate mundane tasks, allowing you to concentrate on higher-value activities.

UNVEILING THE PROJECT MANAGEMENT AI INTEGRATION (PMAI) METHOD

This book introduces the Project Management AI Integration (PMAI) method, a comprehensive framework for seamlessly incorporating AI chatbots into your project management practices.

The PMAI Method Consists of Five Key Stages:

1. **Assess:** Evaluate your organization's current project management processes, tools, and pain points to identify areas where AI chatbots can add value.

2. **Integrate:** Implement an AI chatbot platform that aligns with your organization's needs, ensuring compatibility with existing systems and tools.

3. **Train:** Provide the AI chatbot with relevant data, such as project documentation, process flows, and historical information, to enhance its understanding of your unique environment.

4. **Collaborate:** Foster collaboration between human project managers and the AI chatbot, leveraging their respective strengths for optimal project execution.

5. **Refine:** Continuously monitor and refine the AI chatbot's performance, incorporating feedback and adjusting its algorithms for improved accuracy and efficiency.

INVITING READERS TO REIMAGINE PROJECT MANAGEMENT WITH AI

As you embark on this journey through the pages of this book, be prepared to challenge conventional thinking and embrace a paradigm shift in project management. AI chatbots are not mere tools; they are intelligent partners that can augment your capabilities and drive project success.

Imagine a future where you can effortlessly navigate complex projects, make informed decisions, and deliver exceptional results – all with the support of a virtual assistant that understands your needs and learning preferences.

This book will guide you through real-world case studies, practical examples, and step-by-step implementations, ensuring that you can harness the full potential of AI chatbots in your project management endeavors.

Embrace the future of project management. Unlock the power of AI chatbots and embark on a transformative journey that will redefine how you lead, collaborate, and achieve project excellence.

Get ready to reimagine project management with AI as your co-pilot, soaring to new heights of productivity, efficiency, and success.

To help you assess your readiness for AI adoption in project management, we offer a free online assessment tool. Evaluate your current situation by taking the assessment at: www.rethinkprojectmanagement.com/assessment

1

DISRUPTING PROJECT MANAGEMENT NORMS

CHALLENGE TRADITIONAL PROJECT MANAGEMENT NOTIONS.

In today's rapidly changing business landscape, traditional project management practices are being disrupted. The linear, rigid approaches that worked in the past are no longer sufficient. We must challenge long-held assumptions and embrace new mindsets to thrive in an era of constant change and uncertainty.

Assumption 1: Projects Follow a Predictable Path

For decades, project managers have relied on meticulous planning and a sequential series of steps to deliver projects. The waterfall model, with its defined phases of initiation, planning, execution, monitoring, and closure, was the industry standard. However, this approach assumes that all requirements can be gathered upfront and that the project environment remains stable throughout. In reality, customer needs fluctuate, market conditions shift, and technology evolves rapidly. Sticking rigidly to an outdated plan often leads to delays, excessive rework, and missed opportunities.

The Disruption: Embrace Agility and Iterative Approaches

Agile methodologies, such as Scrum and Kanban, have emerged as a more flexible and adaptive approach to project management. Instead of extensive upfront planning, agile emphasizes incremental development, continuous feedback, and the ability to pivot based on changing requirements. Work is divided into small, manageable increments, allowing teams to deliver value frequently and respond swiftly to new insights or obstacles. This iterative approach increases project transparency, reduces risks, and fosters a culture of continuous improvement.

Assumption 2: Project Managers are Command-and-Control Leaders

Traditionally, project managers were expected to be authoritative leaders who directed teams through a predetermined plan. They were the single point of control, making decisions and delegating tasks to team members. However, this top-down approach can stifle creativity, limit collaboration, and breed an environment of disengagement.

The Disruption: Cultivate Servant Leadership and Self-Organizing Teams

In today's dynamic environment, project managers must transition from command-and-control leaders to servant leaders who empower and enable their teams. Servant leadership focuses on supporting team members, removing obstacles, and creating an environment where individuals can thrive and take ownership of their work. By fostering a culture of trust, transparency, and shared responsibility, project managers can unlock the full potential of their teams.

Moreover, self-organizing teams have emerged as a powerful

disruption to traditional team structures. These cross-functional teams have the autonomy to make decisions, manage their own workload, and hold each other accountable. The project manager's role shifts from micromanaging to facilitating, coaching, and providing strategic guidance. This approach not only increases team engagement and motivation but also fosters a more dynamic and responsive project environment.

Assumption 3: Project Success is Measured by the Triple Constraint

For years, project success has been defined by the "triple constraint" of scope, time, and cost. If a project was delivered within the agreed-upon scope, on time, and within budget, it was deemed successful. However, this narrow definition fails to consider other critical factors, such as customer satisfaction, long-term impact, and organizational benefits.

The Disruption: Redefine Success with a Holistic Perspective

Successful projects should not only meet the triple constraint but also deliver value to stakeholders and align with the organization's strategic objectives. Project managers must shift their focus from merely executing tasks to understanding the broader context and ensuring that project outcomes contribute to the organization's overall mission and goals.

Furthermore, success should be measured beyond the project's completion. The true impact of a project can often be fully realized months or even years after its delivery. Project managers should establish mechanisms to track long-term benefits, gather feedback from end-users, and continuously assess the project's lasting impact on the organization and its customers.

Assumption 4: Projects are Temporary Endeavors

Traditional project management methodologies treat projects as temporary endeavors with a defined start and end date. Once a project is completed, teams disband, and resources are reallocated to new initiatives. This approach can lead to a loss of knowledge, disruption in team dynamics, and a constant cycle of rebuilding.

The Disruption: Foster Continuous Improvement and Knowledge Sharing

In today's fast-paced environment, projects are no longer isolated events but part of a continuous evolution. Organizations must adopt a mindset of continuous improvement, where lessons learned from completed projects are captured and applied to future initiatives. By establishing effective knowledge management systems and fostering a culture of knowledge sharing, organizations can build upon their successes and avoid repeating past mistakes.

Moreover, organizations should explore the concept of persistent teams, where core members remain together and transition seamlessly from one project to the next. This approach can enhance team cohesion, reduce onboarding costs, and accelerate project delivery times.

Assumption 5: Project Managers are Task Managers

Traditionally, project managers were primarily focused on managing tasks, schedules, and budgets. They were responsible for creating detailed plans, tracking progress, and ensuring that work was completed according to predetermined specifications. However, this narrow focus on task management often overlooked the human aspects of project management.

The Disruption: Prioritize People and Emotional Intelligence

Successful project managers in the modern era must prioritize people over tasks. They must possess strong emotional intelligence skills to build trust, foster collaboration, and navigate the complexities of leading diverse teams. Project managers should create an environment where team members feel valued, supported, and motivated to contribute their best efforts.

Furthermore, project managers must develop their coaching and mentoring abilities to support the professional growth of their team members. By investing in people and nurturing their talents, project managers can cultivate a culture of continuous learning, innovation, and personal development, ultimately driving overall organizational success.

Embracing Disruption for Project Management Excellence

Disrupting traditional project management norms is not about abandoning proven practices altogether. Instead, it's about recognizing the limitations of outdated approaches and embracing new mindsets and methodologies that align with the realities of today's fast-paced business environment.

By challenging assumptions, fostering agility, empowering teams, redefining success, promoting continuous improvement, and prioritizing people, project managers can navigate the complexities of modern projects with greater efficiency, effectiveness, and stakeholder satisfaction.

Remember, disruption is not a one-time event but an ongoing journey of adaptation and evolution. Project managers who actively seek out and embrace disruptive practices will not only survive but thrive in an era of constant change, positioning themselves and their organizations as industry leaders.

WHAT ARE TEXT-BASED GENERATIVE AI CHATBOTS?

The project management world is evolving rapidly. Traditional methods that were once considered best practices are now being challenged by new technologies and approaches. One such disruptive force is the emergence of text-based generative AI chatbots, which are poised to become the new normal in project management.

Imagine having a virtual assistant that can understand and communicate in natural language, just like a human. This assistant is powered by cutting-edge artificial intelligence, specifically designed to help project managers streamline their workflows and increase productivity.

Text-based generative AI chatbots are software applications that use natural language processing (NLP) and machine learning to interpret written or spoken input and generate human-like responses. Unlike rule-based chatbots, which have limited pre-programmed responses, generative AI chatbots can understand context, learn from data, and dynamically generate relevant and coherent text.

These chatbots can act as intelligent personal assistants, helping project managers with various tasks, from project planning and risk analysis to document generation and progress tracking.

Disrupting Traditional Project Management Practices

Project management has long been governed by established

methodologies, such as Waterfall, Agile, and Scrum. While these frameworks have proven effective in many cases, they also come with limitations and challenges. Text-based generative AI chatbots have the potential to disrupt these traditional approaches by introducing new levels of efficiency, automation, and adaptability.

1. Enhanced Project Planning and Scope Definition

One of the most significant challenges in project management is accurately defining the scope and creating comprehensive project plans. Text-based generative AI chatbots can assist in breaking down complex requirements, analyzing project details, and generating initial plans and timelines. This can save project managers significant time and effort, allowing them to focus on higher-level tasks.

2. Intelligent Document Analysis and Summarization

Project managers often deal with voluminous documents, such as contracts, specifications, and reports. Manually analyzing and summarizing these documents can be time-consuming and prone to errors. Text-based generative AI chatbots can quickly process these documents, extracting key information and insights, and presenting concise summaries. This can greatly improve decision-making and ensure that critical details are not overlooked.

3. Dynamic Risk Identification and Mitigation

Identifying and mitigating risks is crucial for project success. Traditional risk management approaches often rely on pre-defined templates and checklists, which may not account for unique project circumstances. Text-based generative AI chatbots can analyze project details, historical data, and industry best practices to dynamically identify potential risks and suggest tailored mitigation strategies.

4. Intelligent Task Delegation and Progress Tracking

Effective task delegation and progress tracking are essential for keeping projects on track. Text-based generative AI chatbots can assist project managers in assigning tasks to team members based on their skills, availability, and workload. The chatbots can also track progress, provide updates and reminders, and escalate issues when necessary, ensuring that projects remain on schedule.

5. Automated Status Reporting and Updates

Communicating project status and progress to stakeholders is a critical but often time-consuming task for project managers. Text-based generative AI chatbots can consolidate information from various sources and generate comprehensive status reports, ensuring that stakeholders remain informed and engaged throughout the project lifecycle.

Embracing the New Normal

While the introduction of text-based generative AI chatbots may seem disruptive, it is essential to recognize that disruption is often a catalyst for innovation and progress. As with any new technology, there will be challenges and a learning curve, but the potential benefits are significant.

One of the key advantages of text-based generative AI chatbots is their ability to augment human intelligence, rather than replace it. Project managers can leverage these chatbots to automate repetitive tasks, gain insights, and make more informed decisions, while still maintaining control and oversight over the project.

Moreover, these chatbots can adapt and learn from experience, continuously improving their performance and increasing their value over time. As more project data is fed into the system, the chatbots become more accurate and efficient, creating a virtuous cycle of continuous improvement.

Preparing for the Transition

To successfully embrace text-based generative AI chatbots as the new normal in project management, organizations and individuals must take proactive steps to prepare for this transition.

1. Invest in Training and Upskilling

While text-based generative AI chatbots are designed to be user-friendly, it is essential for project managers and team members to receive proper training on how to effectively interact with and leverage these tools. This may involve learning new skills, such as prompt engineering (crafting effective prompts for the chatbot) and interpreting the chatbot's responses.

2. Establish Clear Guidelines and Governance

As with any new technology, it is crucial to establish clear guidelines and governance around the use of text-based generative AI chatbots. This includes defining the scope of their use, establishing protocols for data privacy and security, and ensuring that the chatbots are used ethically and responsibly.

3. Foster a Culture of Continuous Learning

Embracing text-based generative AI chatbots as the new normal requires a mindset shift towards continuous learning and adaptation. Project managers and team members must be willing to experiment, learn from failures, and continuously refine their approaches to working with these chatbots.

4. Collaborate with Technology Providers

Building a successful partnership with the technology providers of text-based generative AI chatbots is essential. This collaboration should involve open communication, feedback loops, and a shared commitment to continuously improving the chatbots' capabilities to meet the evolving needs of project managers.

The Future of Project Management with AI

As text-based generative AI chatbots become more prevalent in project management, we can expect to see further advancements and innovations in this space. Potential future developments may include:

- Increased integration with other project management tools and platforms, enabling seamless data exchange and workflow optimization.
- Enhanced natural language processing capabilities, allowing for more nuanced and context-aware communication with the chatbots.
- The emergence of specialized chatbots tailored to specific industries or project management methodologies.
- The incorporation of advanced analytics and predictive modeling to provide more accurate risk assessments and project forecasting.

Ultimately, the integration of text-based generative AI chatbots into project management practices represents a significant step towards a more efficient, data-driven, and intelligent approach to managing projects. While change can be daunting, embracing this new normal can unlock new levels of productivity, innovation, and success for project managers and their organizations.

PRESENT PROBLEMS WITH CURRENT PROJECT WORKFLOWS

In today's fast-paced business world, the ability to deliver successful projects is crucial. However, many organizations still follow traditional project management approaches that may not be well-suited for the rapidly changing landscape. Current project workflows often encounter significant challenges that can hinder progress and lead to suboptimal outcomes. It's time to disrupt the conventional norms and address these problems head-on.

Problem 1: Rigid and Inflexible Methodologies

One of the most significant issues with current project workflows is the adherence to rigid methodologies that fail to adapt to the dynamic nature of projects. Many organizations still rely heavily on traditional waterfall approaches, where each phase of the project must be completed before moving on to the next. This linear process can be inflexible and struggle to accommodate changes in requirements, market conditions, or unforeseen circumstances.

In today's rapidly evolving business landscape, projects often need to pivot and adapt quickly. Sticking to a rigid methodology can lead to delays, unnecessary rework, and a lack of agility in responding to changes. Successful project management requires a more flexible and iterative approach that allows for continuous improvement and the ability to adjust course as needed.

Problem 2: Ineffective Communication and Collaboration

Effective communication and collaboration are critical for project success, yet many project workflows suffer from breakdowns in these areas. Siloed teams, lack of transparency, and inefficient information sharing can lead to misunderstandings, missed deadlines, and rework.

In traditional project management settings, communication is often hierarchical and top-down, with information flowing primarily from the project manager to team members. This approach can limit valuable input and feedback from those working directly on the project tasks. Additionally, reliance on lengthy meetings, endless email threads, and disparate communication channels can further hinder collaboration and slow down decision-making processes.

Problem 3: Inadequate Risk Management

Effective risk management is essential for mitigating potential issues that could derail a project. However, many current project workflows lack robust risk identification and mitigation strategies. Often, risk assessment is treated as a one-time exercise during the planning phase, failing to account for the dynamic nature of projects and the ever-changing risk landscape.

Without a continuous and proactive approach to risk management, projects can be blindsided by unforeseen challenges, leading to delays, cost overruns, and potential failure. Project teams may find themselves reactive rather than proactive, scrambling to address issues as they arise rather than anticipating and mitigating them in advance.

Problem 4: Resource Constraints and Inefficient Allocation

Resource management is a pervasive challenge in project management. Many organizations struggle with limited budgets, staffing shortages, and competing priorities, making it difficult to allocate the necessary resources effectively.

Traditional project workflows often rely on manual resource allocation processes, which can be time-consuming and prone to errors. Project managers may spend significant time juggling resource assignments, trying to match the right skills and availability with project tasks. This inefficient allocation can lead to underutilized resources, team member burnout, and missed deadlines.

Problem 5: Lack of Automated Processes and Outdated Tools

In an age where technology is rapidly advancing, many project management workflows still rely heavily on manual processes and outdated tools. From creating project plans and schedules to generating status reports and tracking progress, numerous tasks are often performed manually, leaving room for errors and inefficiencies.

Additionally, many organizations continue to use legacy project management software that may not integrate well with other systems or lack advanced features like artificial intelligence (AI) and automation capabilities. This lack of modern tools can hinder productivity, data-driven decision-making, and the ability to leverage cutting-edge technologies that could streamline project workflows.

Problem 6: Knowledge Silos and Suboptimal Knowledge Sharing

In many organizations, project knowledge and best practices are often siloed within individuals or teams, making it difficult to share and leverage that valuable information across the organization. This issue can lead to reinventing the wheel, repeating mistakes, and missing opportunities to learn from past successes and failures.

Effective knowledge management and sharing are critical for continuous improvement and building organizational capabilities. However, current project workflows may lack robust systems for capturing, organizing, and disseminating project-related knowledge, leading to knowledge silos and suboptimal knowledge sharing.

Problem 7: Stakeholder Misalignment and Expectation Management

Stakeholder management is a crucial aspect of project management, yet many project workflows struggle with aligning stakeholder expectations and ensuring consistent engagement throughout the project lifecycle. Misaligned stakeholders can lead to scope creep, conflicting priorities, and a lack of buy-in, ultimately jeopardizing project success.

Current processes for stakeholder management may be reactive and ad hoc, relying heavily on manual communication channels and infrequent updates. This approach can make it challenging to proactively manage stakeholder expectations, address concerns, and maintain consistent alignment throughout the project's duration.

By addressing these present problems with current project workflows, organizations can pave the way for more successful and efficient project management practices. Embracing disruption and adopting new approaches, tools, and technologies can help project teams overcome these challenges and achieve their desired outcomes more effectively.

The following chapters will explore disruptive ideas, insights, and methodologies that challenge traditional project management norms, offering a fresh perspective on how to transform project workflows and unlock new levels of success.

EXPLORING THE NEED FOR TEXT-BASED GENERATIVE AI CHATBOTS

In today's fast-paced digital world, the technology landscape is rapidly evolving. New tools and methodologies are constantly emerging, driving organizations to adapt swiftly. This relentless pace of change poses significant challenges for professionals, especially project managers tasked with delivering successful outcomes. Amidst this flux, the integration of artificial intelligence (AI) solutions has become vital for streamlining operations and gaining a competitive edge. One such promising AI application is text-based generative chatbots, designed to assist project managers in navigating the complexities of their roles.

The Role of Project Managers in Dynamic Environments

Project managers play a pivotal role in orchestrating teams, resources, and tasks to achieve specific objectives within defined constraints. Their responsibilities span project planning, execution, monitoring, and closure, while ensuring adherence to budgets, timelines, and quality standards. However, in today's dynamic technological landscapes, project managers face numerous obstacles that can impede their path to success.

Some of the key challenges include rapidly evolving technologies, remote and distributed teams, heightened cybersecurity concerns, stringent compliance regulations, and the constant pressure to deliver on time and within budget. Additionally, effective stakeholder management, cross-functional collaboration, and optimal resource allocation often present formidable hurdles. These multifaceted demands underscore the need for innovative solutions that can enhance project managers' productivity, decision-making, and overall effectiveness.

The Potential of Text-Based Generative AI Chatbots

Text-based generative AI chatbots offer a powerful solution to address many of the challenges faced by project managers. These AI-powered conversational assistants can comprehend and generate human-like text, enabling seamless interaction and collaboration. By leveraging natural language processing (NLP) and machine learning algorithms, these chatbots can understand and respond to queries, provide recommendations, and even generate content tailored to specific project management tasks.

One of the primary advantages of text-based generative AI chatbots is their ability to streamline workflows and reduce administrative burdens. For instance, chatbots can assist in project planning by breaking down complex requirements, defining scopes, and creating initial project plans and timelines. This not only saves time but also ensures that critical details are not overlooked, mitigating potential risks from the outset.

Furthermore, chatbots can facilitate effective communication and knowledge sharing within project teams. They can summarize meeting notes, highlighting key action items and decisions, and distribute concise updates to stakeholders. This capability fosters transparency and alignment, essential for successful project execution.

In addition to communication, text-based generative AI chatbots can contribute to document analysis and summarization. Project managers often deal with lengthy contracts, specifications, and reports, which can be time-consuming to review. Chatbots can quickly analyze these documents, extracting pertinent information and insights, enabling project managers to make informed decisions more efficiently.

Risk management is another area where chatbots can prove invaluable. By analyzing project details and historical data, they can identify potential risks and suggest mitigation strategies, helping to create robust contingency plans. This proactive approach can minimize disruptions and ensure projects remain on track.

Task delegation and progress tracking are vital aspects of project management, and chatbots can streamline these processes. Project managers can assign tasks, set deadlines, and receive regular updates from the chatbot, reducing the need for manual follow-ups and increasing overall productivity.

Moreover, chatbots can serve as knowledge repositories, capturing and disseminating project management best practices, lessons learned, and organizational standards. This centralized knowledge base ensures consistent application of proven methodologies and facilitates continuous improvement across projects.

Empowering Project Managers with AI-Driven Insights

Beyond streamlining operational tasks, text-based generative AI chatbots can provide valuable insights and recommendations to project managers. By analyzing project requirements, available resources, and constraints, chatbots can offer suggestions for optimizing resource allocation, ensuring efficient utilization of personnel, budgets, and time.

In the realm of training and onboarding, chatbots can guide new project managers or team members through project management methodologies, tools, and processes specific to the organization. This consistent and accessible training can accelerate the learning curve and promote standardization across teams.

Additionally, chatbots can assist in content generation, such as drafting project proposals, presentations, or reports. While these drafts would require review and refinement by project managers, the initial content creation can save significant time and effort.

Addressing Potential Challenges and Limitations

While text-based generative AI chatbots offer numerous benefits, it is essential to acknowledge and address potential challenges and limitations. One concern is the accuracy and reliability of the information provided by the chatbot, particularly in complex or specialized domains. Ensuring that chatbots are trained on accurate and up-to-date data sources is crucial to mitigate the risk of propagating errors or outdated information.

Another challenge is the potential for bias in the chatbot's responses, which could stem from biases present in the training data or algorithms used. Continuous monitoring and bias testing should be implemented to identify and mitigate such biases, promoting fairness and objectivity in the chatbot's outputs.

Furthermore, the integration of chatbots into existing project management workflows and tools may require careful planning and implementation. Compatibility issues, data sharing protocols, and user adoption challenges must be addressed to ensure seamless integration and maximize the chatbot's effectiveness.

Security and privacy considerations are also paramount when introducing AI-powered chatbots into project management processes. Robust access controls, data encryption, and compliance with relevant regulations (e.g., GDPR, HIPAA) are essential to protect sensitive project information and maintain stakeholder trust.

Embracing the Future of Project Management

As technology continues to evolve at a rapid pace, project managers must adapt and leverage innovative solutions to maintain their competitive edge. Text-based generative AI chatbots present a promising opportunity to enhance project management capabilities, streamline workflows, and drive successful project outcomes.

By embracing these AI-powered assistants, project managers can overcome many of the obstacles they face in today's dynamic technological landscapes. From project planning and risk management to communication and knowledge sharing, chatbots offer a comprehensive suite of capabilities tailored to the unique needs of project managers.

However, it is essential to approach the adoption of chatbots with a strategic mindset, addressing potential challenges related to accuracy, bias, integration, and security. Continuous monitoring, feedback loops, and ongoing improvements will be crucial to maximizing the benefits of these AI-driven solutions.

As the technology landscape continues to transform, the demand for efficient and intelligent project management solutions will only increase. By harnessing the power of text-based generative AI chatbots, project managers can position themselves at the forefront of this digital evolution, delivering successful projects with enhanced productivity, decision-making, and overall effectiveness.

28

2

GAINING INSIGHTS WITH TEXT-BASED GENERATIVE AI CHATBOTS

UNDERSTANDING AI CAPABILITIES IN PROJECT MANAGEMENT

In today's fast-paced and ever-evolving IT landscape, project managers face numerous challenges that can impede their progress toward achieving desired outcomes. From navigating technological advancements and remote work environments to managing resource constraints and stakeholder expectations, the complexities are multifaceted. However, the emergence of text-based generative AI chatbots presents a powerful solution to overcome these obstacles and unlock unprecedented productivity.

These intelligent conversational assistants leverage natural language processing (NLP) and machine learning algorithms, enabling seamless interaction and collaboration with project managers and their teams. By harnessing the capabilities of text-based generative AI chatbots, project managers can streamline workflows, gain valuable insights, and make data-driven decisions, ultimately driving successful project outcomes.

Project Initiation and Planning

One of the critical capabilities of text-based generative AI chatbots is their ability to assist in project initiation and planning. Through natural language interaction, project managers can provide high-level objectives, constraints, and stakeholder requirements to the chatbot. Leveraging its knowledge base and machine learning algorithms, the chatbot can then break down complex tasks, identify dependencies, and create comprehensive project plans, including timelines, resource allocations, and milestones.

This capability not only saves significant time and effort during the planning phase but also ensures that critical details are not overlooked and that project plans align with organizational standards and best practices.

Meeting Summarization and Knowledge Management

Effective communication and knowledge sharing are vital for project success. Text-based generative AI chatbots can streamline these processes by summarizing meeting notes, transcripts, and documents, highlighting key action items, decisions, and insights. Project managers can simply upload or share relevant files, and the chatbot can quickly generate concise summaries, which can be easily distributed to team members and stakeholders.

Furthermore, chatbots can serve as centralized knowledge bases, capturing and disseminating project management best practices, lessons learned, and organizational standards. This capability promotes consistent application of proven methodologies and facilitates continuous learning and improvement across projects.

Risk Identification and Mitigation Strategies

Risk management is a critical aspect of project management, and text-based generative AI chatbots can provide valuable support in this area. By analyzing project details, historical data, and external factors, chatbots can identify potential risks and suggest mitigation strategies. Through natural language interaction, project managers can describe project scenarios or specific concerns, and the chatbot can leverage its risk analysis capabilities to identify potential risks and propose contingency plans.

Task Delegation, Progress Tracking, and Team Coordination

Effective task delegation and progress tracking are essential for maintaining project momentum and ensuring timely completion. Text-based generative AI chatbots can streamline these processes by allowing project managers to assign tasks, set deadlines, and receive regular updates on progress. Through natural language commands or conversational interaction, project managers can delegate tasks to team members, and the chatbot can send reminders, track completion status, and provide real-time updates on progress.

Status Reporting and Stakeholder Communication

Keeping stakeholders informed about project progress, risks, and issues is crucial for maintaining transparency and building trust. Text-based generative AI chatbots can assist in generating comprehensive project status reports by consolidating information from various sources. By analyzing data from project management tools, team communication channels, and other relevant sources, the chatbot can generate clear and concise status reports tailored to specific stakeholder needs.

Resource Allocation and Optimization

Effective resource management is a critical factor in project success. Text-based generative AI chatbots can support this by analyzing project requirements, available resources (including personnel, equipment, and budgets), and constraints. The chatbot can then provide recommendations for optimal resource allocation, minimizing conflicts and ensuring that the right resources are available when needed, reducing potential delays and cost overruns.

Training and Onboarding Support

Text-based generative AI chatbots can assist in training and onboarding new project managers or team members, providing guidance on project management methodologies, tools, and processes specific to the organization. This consistent and accessible training can accelerate the learning curve and promote standardization across teams, ensuring that best practices are consistently applied.

Proposal and Content Generation

Project managers often need to generate various project-related content, such as proposals, presentations, or reports. Text-based generative AI chatbots can assist in this process by leveraging their natural language generation capabilities to create high-quality initial drafts based on provided guidelines, requirements, and project details. While these drafts will require review and refinement, the initial content generation can save significant time and effort, allowing project teams to focus on higher-value tasks and strategic decision-making.

Embracing Text-Based Generative AI Chatbots: Opportunities and Challenges

The integration of text-based generative AI chatbots into project

RETHINK PROJECT MANAGEMENT

management practices offers numerous opportunities for enhancing efficiency, mitigating risks, and driving successful project outcomes. However, it is essential to acknowledge and address potential challenges and limitations.

One challenge is ensuring the accuracy and reliability of the information provided by the chatbot, particularly in complex or specialized domains. Continuously monitoring and updating the chatbot's knowledge base with accurate and up-to-date data sources is crucial to mitigate the risk of propagating errors or outdated information.

Another challenge is the potential for bias in the chatbot's responses, which could stem from biases present in the training data or algorithms used. Implementing bias testing and mitigation strategies is essential to promote fairness and objectivity in the chatbot's outputs.

Furthermore, the integration of chatbots into existing project management workflows and tools may require careful planning and implementation. Compatibility issues, data sharing protocols, and user adoption challenges must be addressed to ensure seamless integration and maximize the chatbot's effectiveness.

Security and privacy considerations are also paramount when introducing AI-powered chatbots into project management processes. Robust access controls, data encryption, and compliance with relevant regulations (e.g., GDPR, HIPAA) are essential to protect sensitive project information and maintain stakeholder trust.

Despite these challenges, the potential benefits of leveraging text-based generative AI chatbots in project management are significant. By embracing these intelligent assistants, project managers can navigate the complexities of the IT landscape, streamline workflows, gain valuable insights, and make more informed decisions, ultimately increasing the likelihood of project success and propelling their careers forward.

As technology continues to evolve, it is crucial for project managers to stay informed about the latest advancements in AI and their applications in project management. Continuous learning, adaptation, and a willingness to embrace innovative solutions will be key to staying ahead in an increasingly competitive and rapidly changing technological landscape.

CASE STUDIES: AI CHATBOTS TRANSFORMING PROJECTS

As project managers navigate the complexities of the modern IT landscape, the adoption of cutting-edge technologies like text-based generative AI chatbots is becoming increasingly vital. These intelligent assistants offer a powerful suite of capabilities that can streamline workflows, enhance productivity, and drive successful project outcomes. Through real-world case studies, we will explore how AI chatbots are transforming the way projects are managed, offering valuable insights into their practical applications.

Case Study 1: Acme Tech Solutions - Accelerating Project Initiation and Planning

Acme Tech Solutions, a leading software development company, faced challenges in efficiently translating complex client requirements into comprehensive project plans. Their project managers often spent weeks analyzing lengthy specifications and stakeholder inputs, delaying project kickoffs.

To address this bottleneck, Acme integrated a text-based generative AI chatbot into their project management processes. Project managers could now provide the chatbot with high-level objectives, constraints, and stakeholder requirements through natural language interaction. Leveraging its knowledge base and machine learning capabilities, the chatbot would then generate detailed project plans, including timelines, resource allocations, and milestones.

The results were remarkable. Project initiation times were reduced by 60%, allowing Acme to respond more quickly to client needs. Project managers could focus on higher-value tasks, such as stakeholder engagement and risk mitigation, while the chatbot handled the intricacies of project planning.

Case Study 2: GlobalTech Inc. - Enhancing Risk Management and Mitigation

GlobalTech Inc., a multinational IT services provider, recognized the importance of proactive risk management in delivering successful projects. However, their project managers often struggled to identify potential risks and develop contingency plans amidst the complexities of large-scale projects.

To address this challenge, GlobalTech implemented a text-based generative AI chatbot that could analyze project details, historical data, and external factors to identify potential risks. Project managers could describe specific project scenarios or concerns through natural language interaction, and the chatbot would leverage its risk analysis capabilities to provide comprehensive risk assessments and suggest mitigation strategies.

This integration proved invaluable, particularly in navigating regulatory compliance and cybersecurity risks, which are critical in the IT industry. Project managers could make more informed decisions, mitigating risks proactively and minimizing potential disruptions or delays.

Case Study 3: InnovaTech - Streamlining Team Coordination and Progress Tracking

InnovaTech, a rapidly growing fintech startup, faced challenges in coordinating and tracking progress across multiple agile development teams working on a large-scale project. With teams distributed across different locations, ensuring effective communication, task delegation, and progress monitoring became increasingly complex.

To address these challenges, InnovaTech implemented a text-based generative AI chatbot that could streamline team coordination and progress tracking. Project managers could assign tasks to team members, set deadlines, and receive regular updates on progress through natural language commands or conversational interaction.

The chatbot proved instrumental in maintaining project momentum, sending reminders, tracking completion status, and providing real-time updates on progress. Team members could easily stay informed and aligned, reducing the need for frequent status meetings and increasing overall productivity.

Case Study 4: TechXperts - Automating Reporting and Stakeholder Communication

TechXperts, a leading IT consulting firm, recognized the importance of transparent and effective stakeholder communication in fostering trust and ensuring project success. However, their project managers often struggled to consolidate information from multiple sources and generate comprehensive status reports in a timely manner.

To address this challenge, TechXperts adopted a text-based generative AI chatbot capable of analyzing data from project management tools, team communication channels, and other relevant sources. The chatbot could then generate clear and concise status reports tailored to specific stakeholder needs, providing updates on progress, risks, issues, and upcoming milestones.

This automation not only saved significant time and effort for project managers but also ensured that stakeholders received consistent and up-to-date information, allowing them to make informed decisions and provide timely feedback.

These case studies illustrate the transformative impact of text-based generative AI chatbots on project management practices across various industries and project types. By leveraging the capabilities of these intelligent assistants, project managers can overcome common obstacles, streamline workflows, and unlock unprecedented productivity.

Challenges and Best Practices

While the benefits of adopting AI chatbots are significant, it is essential to acknowledge and address potential challenges and limitations to ensure successful integration and maximize their effectiveness.

One key challenge is ensuring the accuracy and reliability of the information provided by the chatbot, particularly in complex or specialized domains. Continuously monitoring and updating the chatbot's knowledge base with accurate and up-to-date data sources is crucial to mitigate the risk of propagating errors or outdated information.

Another challenge is the potential for bias in the chatbot's responses, which could stem from biases present in the training data or algorithms used. Implementing bias testing and mitigation strategies is essential to promote fairness and objectivity in the chatbot's outputs.

Security and privacy considerations are also paramount when introducing AI-powered chatbots into project management processes. Robust access controls, data encryption, and compliance with relevant regulations (e.g., GDPR, HIPAA) are essential to protect sensitive project information and maintain stakeholder trust.

To address these challenges and ensure successful adoption, project managers should follow best practices such as:

1. Clearly define the chatbot's scope and intended use cases to align with organizational needs and project management processes.
2. Invest in training and onboarding to ensure seamless integration and user adoption.
3. Establish clear governance and oversight mechanisms to monitor the chatbot's performance and outputs.
4. Continuously update and refine the chatbot's knowledge base with the latest industry standards, best practices, and organizational learnings.
5. Implement robust security measures, including access controls, data encryption, and regular security audits.
6. Encourage a culture of continuous learning and adaptation within the organization to embrace new technologies and innovations effectively.

By following these best practices and addressing potential challenges proactively, project managers can leverage the full potential of text-based generative AI chatbots, driving innovation and transforming project management practices for sustained success.

INSIGHTS INTO FUTURE PROJECT MANAGEMENT TRENDS INFLUENCED BY TEXT-BASED GENERATIVE AI CHATBOTS

The integration of text-based generative AI chatbots into project management practices is poised to reshape the landscape of the IT industry. As these intelligent assistants become more sophisticated and prevalent, they will inevitably influence and drive several key trends in the way projects are managed and executed. In this chapter, we will explore the potential impact of AI chatbots on future project management trends, providing insights into the transformative changes that lie ahead.

Trend 1: Accelerated Project Initiation and Planning

One of the most significant effects of AI chatbots will be the streamlining of project initiation and planning processes. These chatbots can rapidly analyze complex project requirements, stakeholder inputs, and organizational constraints to generate comprehensive project plans, timelines, and resource allocations. This capability will dramatically reduce the time and effort required for project managers to translate high-level objectives into actionable plans, allowing for faster project kickoffs and more efficient use of resources.

Trend 2: Enhanced Risk Management and Mitigation

As projects become increasingly complex, the ability to identify and mitigate risks proactively will become paramount. AI chatbots, with their advanced analytical capabilities, can continuously monitor project data, external factors, and historical patterns to detect potential risks and recommend mitigation strategies. This will enable project managers to stay ahead of potential issues, minimizing disruptions and increasing the likelihood of successful project delivery.

Trend 3: Optimized Resource Allocation and Utilization

Efficient resource allocation and utilization are critical for project success, especially in environments with limited budgets and personnel. AI chatbots can analyze project requirements, resource availability, and team member skills to provide data-driven recommendations for optimal resource allocation. This will help project managers maximize resource utilization, ensuring that the right resources are assigned to the right tasks at the right time.

Trend 4: Automated Progress Tracking and Reporting

Keeping stakeholders informed about project progress is a crucial responsibility for project managers. AI chatbots can automate this process by consolidating data from various sources, such as project management tools, communication channels, and team updates, to generate comprehensive status reports. These reports can be tailored to specific stakeholder needs, providing transparent and up-to-date information without requiring significant manual effort from project managers.

Trend 5: Knowledge Management and Continuous Improvement

Effective knowledge management is essential for organizations to learn from past projects and continuously improve their processes. AI chatbots can serve as dynamic repositories of project management best practices, lessons learned, and organizational standards. This knowledge base can be continuously updated and disseminated to project teams, fostering an environment of continuous learning and improvement.

Trend 6: Augmented Team Collaboration and Communication

Effective collaboration and communication within project teams are critical for success, especially in remote or distributed environments. AI chatbots can facilitate seamless communication by summarizing meetings, highlighting key decisions and action items, and providing real-time updates on task progress. This will help ensure that team members stay aligned and informed, reducing the need for frequent meetings and increasing overall productivity.

Trend 7: Personalized Training and Onboarding

Onboarding new team members and providing ongoing training can be time-consuming and resource-intensive processes. AI chatbots can streamline these efforts by providing personalized training and guidance on project management methodologies, tools, and processes specific to the organization. This will enable project managers to quickly upskill their teams and ensure consistent adherence to established best practices.

Trend 8: Automated Content Generation

Project managers often spend significant time creating various types of project-related content, such as proposals, presentations, and reports. AI chatbots can assist in this process by generating initial drafts based on provided inputs and guidelines. Project managers can then review and refine these drafts, saving valuable time and effort while ensuring consistency and quality.

Trend 9: Increased Focus on Strategic Leadership

As AI chatbots take on more operational tasks, project managers will have the opportunity to shift their focus towards strategic leadership and decision-making. They can concentrate on high-level planning, stakeholder management, risk mitigation, and driving innovation, while the chatbot handles more routine tasks and provides data-driven insights to support informed decision-making.

Trend 10: Greater Emphasis on Soft Skills

With AI chatbots handling many technical and operational aspects of project management, the importance of soft skills for project managers will become increasingly pronounced. Skills such as emotional intelligence, communication, change management, and leadership will be crucial for effectively collaborating with teams, managing stakeholder expectations, and driving organizational change initiatives.

While these trends highlight the potential benefits and transformative impact of AI chatbots, it is essential to acknowledge that their adoption will also present challenges and considerations. Project managers and organizations will need to address issues such as data privacy, security, and ethical concerns surrounding AI-driven decision-making. Additionally, the successful integration of AI chatbots will require a cultural shift, with organizations embracing a mindset of continuous learning and adaptation to new technologies.

To navigate these challenges and maximize the benefits of AI chatbots, project managers should focus on developing a deep understanding of the technology's capabilities and limitations. They should also prioritize fostering a culture of innovation and open-mindedness within their teams, encouraging active participation in the integration and refinement of these AI-powered tools.

Furthermore, project managers must remain vigilant in overseeing the outputs and recommendations provided by AI chatbots, ensuring that they align with organizational goals, ethical standards, and regulatory requirements. Regular audits, bias testing, and ongoing refinement of the chatbot's knowledge base will be crucial to maintaining the integrity and reliability of the system.

By embracing these trends and addressing potential challenges proactively, project managers can leverage the power of text-based generative AI chatbots to unlock new levels of efficiency, productivity, and strategic impact. The future of project management in the IT industry will be shaped by the seamless integration of human expertise and AI-driven insights, paving the way for unprecedented success and innovation.

ETHICAL CONSIDERATIONS AND THE HUMAN TOUCH IN AI INTEGRATION

As organizations embrace the integration of text-based generative AI chatbots into project management practices, it is imperative to consider the ethical implications of this technological advancement. While these intelligent assistants offer numerous benefits in enhancing productivity, streamlining processes, and driving innovation, their implementation must be guided by a strong ethical framework to ensure responsible and trustworthy use.

Ethical Consideration 1: Transparency and Accountability

One of the primary ethical concerns surrounding AI chatbots is the potential lack of transparency and accountability in their decision-making processes. These systems are trained on vast amounts of data, and their algorithms can be opaque, making it difficult to understand how they arrive at certain conclusions or recommendations. Project managers must ensure that the chatbot's decision-making processes are transparent, explainable, and auditable. This could involve implementing mechanisms for traceability, allowing stakeholders to understand the reasoning behind the chatbot's outputs and recommendations.

Ethical Consideration 2: Bias and Fairness

AI systems can inadvertently perpetuate or amplify biases present in the data they are trained on, leading to unfair or discriminatory outcomes. This is particularly concerning in project management, where impartial decision-making and resource allocation are crucial. Project managers should work closely with AI developers and subject matter experts to identify and mitigate potential biases in the chatbot's knowledge base and algorithms. Regular bias testing and continuous refinement of the chatbot's training data and models are essential to promote fairness and equity.

Ethical Consideration 3: Data Privacy and Security

The integration of AI chatbots in project management may involve the handling and processing of sensitive organizational data, including project details, stakeholder information, and confidential documents. Project managers must ensure that robust data privacy and security measures are in place to protect this information from unauthorized access or misuse. This includes adhering to relevant data protection regulations, implementing strict access controls, and regularly auditing the chatbot's data handling practices.

Ethical Consideration 4: Human Oversight and Control

While AI chatbots can automate many tasks and provide valuable insights, it is crucial to maintain human oversight and control over critical decision-making processes. Project managers should not blindly accept the chatbot's recommendations but rather use them as inputs to inform their decision-making. They should also have the ability to override or adjust the chatbot's outputs when necessary, based on their professional judgment, experience, and contextual understanding of the project.

Ethical Consideration 5: Responsible Use and Ethical Training

Project managers must ensure that the AI chatbot is used responsibly and in alignment with the organization's ethical principles and values. This includes providing ethical training to team members on the appropriate use of the chatbot, setting clear boundaries on its capabilities and limitations, and establishing guidelines for human oversight and intervention.

While addressing these ethical considerations is essential, it is equally important to acknowledge and leverage the human touch that project managers bring to their roles. AI chatbots, despite their advanced capabilities, cannot fully replicate the nuanced decision-making, emotional intelligence, and leadership skills that successful project managers possess.

The Human Touch in AI Integration

1. **Strategic Vision and Direction:** Project managers play a vital role in setting the strategic vision and direction for their projects, aligning them with the organization's overall goals

and objectives. While AI chatbots can provide data-driven insights and recommendations, the human touch is crucial in translating these insights into a cohesive, long-term strategy that considers broader organizational context and stakeholder interests.

2. **Effective Communication and Stakeholder Management:** Successful project management relies heavily on effective communication, relationship building, and stakeholder management. Project managers must navigate complex interpersonal dynamics, manage expectations, and foster trust and collaboration among diverse stakeholders. While AI chatbots can assist with communication tasks, such as generating reports and summarizing meetings, the human touch is essential in interpreting non-verbal cues, exercising emotional intelligence, and building authentic connections with stakeholders.

3. **Adaptive Leadership and Change Management:** Projects often encounter unforeseen challenges, requiring adaptive leadership and effective change management. Project managers must be prepared to pivot, make tough decisions, and guide their teams through periods of uncertainty and change. AI chatbots can provide valuable risk analysis and contingency planning support, but the human touch is necessary to inspire trust, motivate teams, and navigate the emotional and psychological aspects of change.

4. **Mentoring and Team Development:** Successful project managers not only deliver projects but also invest in the growth and development of their team members. They serve as mentors, provide coaching and feedback, and create opportunities for team members to learn and develop new skills. While AI chatbots can offer training and onboarding

assistance, the human touch in mentoring and fostering a positive team culture is invaluable.

5. **Ethical Decision-Making:** As discussed earlier, ethical considerations are crucial in the integration of AI chatbots. Project managers must exercise ethical judgment, uphold organizational values, and ensure that the chatbot's outputs and recommendations align with ethical principles. The human touch is essential in navigating complex ethical dilemmas, weighing trade-offs, and making principled decisions that consider the broader societal impact.

To successfully integrate AI chatbots into project management practices, organizations must strike a balance between leveraging the capabilities of these intelligent assistants and preserving the human touch that project managers bring to their roles. This balance can be achieved through a collaborative approach, where project managers work in tandem with AI chatbots, leveraging their respective strengths and mitigating their limitations.

One effective approach is to establish a clear division of responsibilities, where AI chatbots handle more routine, data-driven tasks, such as document analysis, risk identification, and progress tracking, while project managers focus on strategic decision-making, stakeholder engagement, team leadership, and ethical oversight. Regular interactions between project managers and the chatbot can facilitate knowledge sharing, continuous improvement, and the refinement of the chatbot's capabilities based on human feedback and domain expertise.

Additionally, organizations should invest in training and upskilling their project managers to work effectively with AI chatbots. This includes developing an understanding of the chatbot's capabilities and limitations, learning how to interpret and critically evaluate its outputs, and fostering a mindset of continuous learning and adaptation to new technologies.

By embracing both the ethical considerations and the human touch in AI integration, organizations can unlock the transformative potential of text-based generative AI chatbots while maintaining the essential human elements that underpin successful project management. This balanced approach will not only drive productivity and efficiency but also foster trust, ethical decision-making, and a culture of innovation and continuous improvement within the IT industry.

Experience the power of text-based generative AI chatbots firsthand by trying out our ProjectPal GPT. Visit: www.rethinkprojectmanagement.com

3

THE PMAI METHOD IN ACTION

The PMAI Method provides a framework for integrating AI chatbots into your project management processes. Using these intelligent assistants, you can increase productivity, efficiency, and project success throughout the whole project lifecycle.

This chapter explores the ten key components of the PMAI Method. Each component is designed to utilize the strengths of AI chatbots while supporting your role as the strategic project leader. From defining project scope and creating comprehensive plans, to optimizing resource allocation, tracking progress, and ensuring adherence to standards - the AI assistant partners with you in navigating complex projects.

You will gain practical insights into how this human-AI collaboration can streamline workflows, reduce risks, improve decision-making, and create an environment of continuous learning in your organization. Real-world examples will illustrate the transformative potential of integrating AI capabilities into your approach to project management.

Whether you are an experienced professional or new to AI, this chapter provides a roadmap for using the PMAI Method. It empowers you to adopt cutting-edge technologies while maintaining control over critical processes. Get ready to revolutionize how you plan, execute, and deliver projects, driving your team to unprecedented levels of achievement.

1. DEFINE AND PLAN WITH AI (D&P)

As a project manager in today's fast-paced IT industry, you know that success often hinges on the crucial first step: defining the project scope and creating a detailed plan. However, sifting through complex requirements, identifying key objectives, and mapping out a comprehensive timeline can be a daunting task, especially when facing tight deadlines and resource constraints.

This is where the PMAI Method and its powerful AI assistant come into play. The Define and Plan (D&P) component harnesses the capabilities of the AI chatbot, allowing you to navigate the project initiation phase with ease and precision.

Breaking Down Complex Requirements

The journey begins with the AI chatbot's ability to deconstruct intricate project requirements into manageable pieces. By feeding the chatbot with relevant documents, such as stakeholder requests, technical specifications, or business objectives, it can quickly analyze and synthesize the information.

The chatbot then presents you with a clear, structured breakdown of the key components, objectives, and deliverables required for the project. This granular understanding ensures that no critical aspect is overlooked, laying a solid foundation for accurate scope definition.

Defining Project Scope with Clarity

Armed with the distilled requirements, you can collaborate with the AI assistant to meticulously define the project's scope. The chatbot prompts you with insightful questions, helping you clarify goals, identify potential risks, and establish boundaries.

For instance, it may ask you to prioritize objectives, considering factors like strategic impact, resource availability, and customer needs. Through this interactive process, the chatbot guides you in shaping a well-defined project scope that aligns with organizational priorities and stakeholder expectations.

Creating Comprehensive Plans

With the scope firmly established, the next step is to develop a detailed project plan. Here, the AI chatbot proves invaluable by breaking down the project into manageable tasks and subtasks. It takes into account dependencies, resource availability, and any identified risks, creating a logical sequence of activities.

You can provide input on task duration estimates, resource requirements, and milestone targets, and the chatbot will seamlessly incorporate these elements into the plan. The result is a comprehensive project roadmap, complete with timelines, resource allocations, and contingency measures.

Iterative Refinement and Stakeholder Alignment

Effective project planning is an iterative process, and the AI assistant excels at facilitating this iterative refinement. As you review the initial plan, you can provide feedback, and the chatbot will adjust the tasks, timelines, and resource allocations accordingly.

Furthermore, the chatbot can generate visual representations of the plan, such as Gantt charts or PERT diagrams, making it easier for you to communicate the project's scope and timeline to stakeholders. This visual aid ensures stakeholder alignment and buy-in from the outset, minimizing the risk of scope creep or misaligned expectations later in the project lifecycle.

SHELDON ST. CLAIR

Continuous Learning and Knowledge Capture

One of the key advantages of the PMAI Method's Define and Plan (D&P) component is its ability to capture and retain knowledge. As you engage with the AI chatbot, it records your decision-making process, rationale, and any lessons learned during the planning phase.

This valuable information is stored in the chatbot's knowledge base, creating an ever-growing repository of project planning best practices specific to your organization. Over time, this knowledge base becomes a powerful asset, enabling the chatbot to provide more insightful recommendations and streamlining the planning process for future projects.

By leveraging the AI assistant's capabilities during the Define and Plan phase, you can overcome common obstacles faced by project managers, such as scope creep, resource constraints, and stakeholder misalignment. The chatbot acts as a virtual co-pilot, guiding you through the complexities of project initiation with precision, efficiency, and continuous learning.

As you embark on your next IT project, embrace the power of the PMAI Method's Define and Plan (D&P) component. With the AI chatbot by your side, you can confidently navigate the project initiation phase, setting the stage for successful execution and delivery.

A Prompt for You To Try:

Prompt Name:	Project Scope and Planning Assistant
Purpose:	Define project scope and create a comprehensive plan with timelines and resource allocation.
Prompt:	Your task is to review the provided project requirements and objectives, and generate a well-defined project scope and detailed plan. The plan should include a breakdown of tasks and subtasks, estimated timelines, resource allocation (including team member assignments), and identified risks or dependencies. Incorporate any specific constraints or stakeholder requirements provided. Present the plan in a clear and organized manner, using appropriate formatting such as Gantt charts or PERT diagrams.

2. SUMMARIZE AND FOCUS USING AI (S&F)

As an IT project manager, staying focused on the core objectives amidst the chaos of competing priorities is crucial. With multiple meetings, numerous documents, and a steady stream of updates, it's easy to lose sight of what truly matters. This is where the "Summarize and Focus" (S&F) component of the PMAI Method comes into play, harnessing the power of AI to keep you and your team laser-focused on the goals that drive project success.

Meeting Summaries at Your Fingertips

Meetings are integral to project management, serving as platforms for collaboration, decision-making, and alignment. However, the sheer volume of information exchanged during these sessions can be overwhelming, making it challenging to capture and act upon the most critical points. This is where the AI assistant steps in, offering a game-changing solution.

By simply uploading the meeting transcripts or notes, the AI assistant can swiftly analyze the content and generate concise summaries. These summaries highlight the key decisions made, action items assigned, and any critical information that requires your attention. No more sifting through lengthy transcripts or worrying about missing vital details – the AI assistant does the heavy lifting, ensuring you stay focused on the most pertinent outcomes.

Distilling Complex Documents into Actionable Insights

Project documentation is often extensive, spanning specifications, contracts, reports, and more. Navigating through this sea of information can be daunting, especially when you need to extract specific insights or make time-sensitive decisions. The AI assistant streamlines this process, acting as your personal document analyst.

By ingesting these documents, the AI assistant can quickly identify the most relevant sections, distill the information into clear and concise summaries, and present you with the actionable insights you need. Whether it's understanding the implications of a contractual clause, identifying potential risks buried within a technical report, or extracting critical requirements from a specification document, the AI assistant ensures you remain focused on the most pressing matters.

Maintaining Momentum with Highlighted Action Items

Amidst the flurry of activities and constant influx of information, it's easy to lose track of the specific tasks and action items that demand your attention. The AI assistant acts as a vigilant sentinel, continuously monitoring and tracking these crucial elements.

By analyzing meeting summaries, project updates, and other relevant communications, the AI assistant can identify and highlight the action items assigned to you or your team. It can then provide timely reminders and updates, ensuring these tasks remain top-of-mind and preventing them from falling through the cracks. This focused approach keeps your team's momentum strong, propelling the project forward without losing sight of critical milestones.

Aligning Team Focus with Centralized Communication

Clear and consistent communication is the lifeblood of any successful project. However, with multiple stakeholders, distributed teams, and various communication channels, it's easy for crucial information to become fragmented or lost in the noise.

The AI assistant addresses this challenge by serving as a centralized communication hub. It can consolidate updates, decisions, and action items from various sources – emails, instant messages, project management tools, and more – into a single, coherent stream. By highlighting the most pertinent information and filtering out the noise, the AI assistant ensures that you and your team remain focused on the same priorities, fostering alignment and shared understanding.

In the fast-paced and complex world of IT project management, maintaining focus is a constant battle. The "Summarize and Focus" component of the PMAI Method, powered by AI, provides a potent solution to this challenge. By leveraging the AI assistant's capabilities in meeting summarization, document analysis, action item tracking, and centralized communication, you can stay laser-focused on the objectives that truly matter. This heightened focus not only increases productivity but also enhances decision-making, fosters team alignment, and ultimately propels your projects towards a successful completion.

A Prompt for You To Try:

Prompt Name:	Meeting AI Assistant
Purpose:	Distil meetings into concise summaries including discussion topics, key takeaways, and action items.
Prompt:	Your task is to review the provided meeting notes and create a concise summary that captures the essential information, focusing on key takeaways and action items assigned to specific individuals or departments during the meeting. Use clear and professional language, and organize the summary in a logical manner using appropriate formatting such as headings, subheadings, and bullet points. Ensure that the summary is easy to understand and provides a comprehensive but succinct overview of the meeting's content, with a particular focus on clearly indicating who is responsible for each action item.

3. ANALYZE AND INSIGHT THROUGH AI (A&I)

As a project manager, you often find yourself inundated with large volumes of project documentation – requirements, specifications, contracts, reports, and more. Sifting through these lengthy documents to extract crucial information and actionable insights can be a daunting and time-consuming task. However, by leveraging the power of AI through the Analyze and Insight (A&I) component of the PMAI Method, you can streamline this process, saving valuable time and effort.

The A&I component harnesses the analytical capabilities of an AI chatbot to parse through extensive project documentation, condense it, and surface key information and insights. This not only enhances your understanding of the project but also enables you to make more informed decisions, mitigate risks, and drive the project forward more effectively.

Here's how the A&I component works:

Step 1: Document Ingestion

The first step is to provide the AI chatbot with the relevant project documents. This can be done by uploading PDF files, sharing links to online documents, or even copy-pasting text directly into the chatbot interface. The chatbot's advanced natural language processing capabilities allow it to understand and analyze various document formats seamlessly.

Step 2: Comprehensive Analysis

Once the documents are ingested, the AI chatbot conducts a thorough analysis, breaking down the content into its components and extracting key elements such as objectives, requirements, constraints, risks, and dependencies. It also identifies and highlights important dates, milestones, and deadlines.

Step 3: Summarization and Insights

After the analysis, the chatbot generates concise summaries of the documents, distilling the essential information into easy-to-digest formats. Additionally, it provides actionable insights by identifying potential risks, areas of concern, and opportunities for optimization or improvement.

Step 4: Interactive Exploration

The A&I component offers an interactive experience, allowing you to engage with the chatbot and explore the analyzed information further. You can ask follow-up questions, seek clarification, or request additional details on specific aspects of the project. The chatbot responds in real-time, providing you with the information you need to make informed decisions.

Step 5: Integration and Collaboration

The insights and summaries generated by the A&I component can be seamlessly integrated into your project management workflows. You can share them with your team, stakeholders, or clients, fostering collaboration and ensuring everyone is aligned with the project's objectives and priorities.

By leveraging the A&I component, you can unlock several benefits:

1. **Time Savings:** The chatbot's ability to quickly analyze and summarize lengthy documents saves you significant time that would otherwise be spent manually sifting through the content.

2. **Improved Decision-Making:** With concise summaries and actionable insights, you can make more informed decisions, mitigating risks and maximizing the chances of project success.

3. **Enhanced Communication:** By sharing the chatbot's summaries and insights with your team and stakeholders, you can ensure everyone is on the same page, improving communication and collaboration.

4. **Continuous Learning:** The chatbot's analysis can uncover

areas where additional knowledge or training may be required, enabling you and your team to address skill gaps proactively.

5. **Risk Mitigation:** The chatbot's ability to identify potential risks early in the project lifecycle allows you to develop mitigation strategies and contingency plans, minimizing the impact of unforeseen challenges.

To illustrate the power of the A&I component, let's consider a scenario where you're tasked with managing a complex software development project. The project documentation includes hundreds of pages of requirements, technical specifications, and legal contracts. Manually analyzing these documents would be a daunting task, but with the AI chatbot, you can:

1. Upload all the relevant documents to the chatbot interface.
2. Have the chatbot analyze the content and generate concise summaries, highlighting key requirements, technical constraints, and legal obligations.
3. Ask the chatbot to identify potential risks based on the analysis, such as dependencies on third-party software or stringent security requirements.
4. Explore specific areas further by engaging with the chatbot through follow-up questions, gaining deeper insights into the project's complexities.
5. Share the summaries and insights with your development team, ensuring everyone understands the project's scope, objectives, and potential challenges.

By leveraging the A&I component, you can streamline the analysis process, gain a comprehensive understanding of the project, and make informed decisions that drive success, all while saving valuable time and effort.

The Analyze and Insight component of the PMAI Method is a powerful tool that empowers project managers to harness the capabilities of AI, enhancing their ability to navigate complex projects and deliver exceptional results. By integrating this component into your project management workflows, you can unlock new levels of productivity, efficiency, and success.

A Prompt for You To Try:

Prompt Name:	Project Document Analysis Assistant
Purpose:	Analyze project documentation and surface key information and insights.
Prompt:	Your task is to review the provided project documents (e.g., requirements, specifications, contracts, reports) and generate concise summaries highlighting the essential information, potential risks or concerns, and opportunities for optimization or improvement. Identify and highlight important dates, milestones, deadlines, and any dependencies. Present the summaries and insights in a clear and organized manner, using appropriate formatting such as bullet points or tables.

4. RISK AND STRATEGY WITH AI SUPPORT (R&S)

One of the most critical aspects of project management is identifying potential risks and proactively developing strategies to mitigate them. Effective risk management can mean the difference between a successful project delivery and one that faces delays, budget overruns, or even failure.

In today's fast-paced IT industry, project managers often find themselves juggling multiple projects, each with its own set of complexities and risks. From technological integration challenges to resource constraints and changing requirements, the list of potential roadblocks can seem endless.

However, by leveraging the capabilities of an AI chatbot through the PMAI (Project Management AI Integration) Method's Risk and Strategy (R&S) component, project managers can navigate these challenges more effectively.

Risk Identification and Analysis

The first step in effective risk management is identifying potential risks. This process can be time-consuming and prone to oversight, especially in complex projects with multiple moving parts. Enter the AI chatbot.

By providing the chatbot with project details, including scope, timelines, resource allocations, and stakeholder requirements, it can analyze this information and flag potential risks. The chatbot's ability to process vast amounts of data and identify patterns that humans might miss can be invaluable in this initial risk identification stage.

For example, the chatbot might identify risks related to dependencies on external vendors, potential regulatory changes that could impact the project, or even resource constraints based on historical data from similar projects.

Mitigation Strategy Development

Once risks have been identified, the next step is to develop strategies to mitigate or manage them. This is where the AI chatbot's analytical capabilities truly shine.

Drawing upon its vast knowledge base and the specific project details, the chatbot can suggest mitigation strategies tailored to the identified risks. These strategies might include contingency plans, risk transference through contracts or insurance, or process adjustments to address potential bottlenecks.

For instance, if the chatbot flags a risk related to a key team member's potential departure, it might suggest cross-training other team members or bringing in temporary resources to ensure knowledge transfer and continuity.

Continuous Risk Monitoring

Risk management is an ongoing process, and the AI chatbot can play a crucial role in continuous monitoring and adjustment. As the project progresses, the chatbot can track key indicators and provide real-time updates on risk levels.

If a previously identified risk escalates or a new risk emerges, the chatbot can alert the project manager, enabling prompt action. This proactive approach helps ensure that risks are addressed before they can significantly impact the project.

Additionally, the chatbot can integrate with project management tools and data sources, providing a comprehensive view of risk across multiple projects and portfolios. This bird's-eye perspective can help project managers prioritize their risk management efforts and allocate resources accordingly.

Leveraging Historical Data and Best Practices

One of the significant advantages of integrating an AI chatbot into the risk management process is its ability to learn from historical data and industry best practices.

As the chatbot is exposed to more projects and their associated risks, it can refine its risk identification and mitigation strategies, becoming increasingly accurate and valuable over time. This continuous learning process ensures that the chatbot's recommendations are based on the most up-to-date and relevant information.

Furthermore, the chatbot can serve as a repository for risk management best practices, capturing lessons learned from past projects and making them easily accessible to project managers. This knowledge sharing can help prevent the repetition of past mistakes and promote the adoption of proven risk management techniques across the organization.

Enhancing Collaboration and Communication

Effective risk management often involves collaboration among various stakeholders, including project teams, subject matter experts, and senior leadership. The AI chatbot can facilitate this collaboration by generating clear and concise risk reports that can be shared with all parties involved.

These reports can include risk assessments, mitigation strategies, and progress updates, ensuring that everyone stays informed and aligned. The chatbot can also assist in scheduling risk review meetings and capturing action items, further streamlining the communication and decision-making processes.

By leveraging the PMAI Method's Risk and Strategy (R&S) component, project managers can harness the power of AI to enhance their risk management capabilities. From identifying potential risks to developing tailored mitigation strategies and continuously monitoring risk levels, the AI chatbot becomes an invaluable ally in navigating the complexities of modern IT projects.

As technology continues to evolve and project complexities increase, the ability to effectively manage risks will become increasingly crucial for project success. By embracing the PMAI Method and integrating AI support into their risk management processes, project managers can stay ahead of the curve, deliver projects more reliably, and ultimately achieve their desired outcomes.

A Prompt for You To Try:

Prompt Name:	Risk Identification and Mitigation Assistant
Purpose:	Identify potential risks and develop tailored mitigation strategies.
Prompt:	Your task is to analyze the provided project details, including scope, timelines, resource allocations, and stakeholder requirements, and identify potential risks that could impact the project's success. For each identified risk, suggest appropriate mitigation strategies or contingency plans. Present the risks and mitigation strategies in a clear and organized manner, using appropriate formatting such as a risk register or a matrix.

5. DELEGATE AND TRACK BY AI (D&T)

As a project manager in today's fast-paced IT industry, you have to juggle many moving parts. With complex projects involving numerous tasks and team members, staying on top of everything can quickly become overwhelming. However, the PMAI (Project Management AI Integration) Method is here to lend a helping hand, particularly with the Delegate and Track (D&T) component.

The Delegate and Track aspect of the PMAI Method allows you to leverage the power of an AI chatbot assistant to streamline task delegation, progress monitoring, and team coordination. By offloading these crucial responsibilities to the AI, you can free up valuable time and mental energy to focus on strategic planning, risk management, and driving your projects toward successful completion.

Task Delegation Made Easy

One of the primary challenges project managers face is effectively delegating tasks to their team members. With the AI chatbot, this process becomes more straightforward and efficient. You can provide the chatbot with a list of tasks, along with details such as deadlines, priorities, and any relevant context.

The AI will then intelligently assign these tasks to the appropriate team members based on their skills, availability, and current workload. This not only saves you time but also ensures that tasks are allocated optimally, reducing the risk of overburdening certain team members while underutilizing others.

Progress Tracking and Reminders

Once tasks have been delegated, the AI chatbot takes on the role of a tireless progress tracker. It continuously monitors the status of each task, gathering updates from team members and consolidating this information into a centralized dashboard.

With a quick glance, you can immediately identify any potential bottlenecks or delays, allowing you to take proactive measures to course-correct before issues escalate. The chatbot can even send automated reminders to team members as deadlines approach, ensuring everyone stays on track and accountable.

Seamless Team Coordination

Effective collaboration is essential for project success, but it can be challenging to coordinate team members working across different time zones or locations. The AI chatbot acts as a central communication hub, facilitating seamless interactions and ensuring everyone is on the same page.

Team members can provide status updates, ask questions, or share information directly with the chatbot, which then disseminates this information to the relevant parties. This streamlined communication process minimizes the need for lengthy email threads or scattered messaging, reducing the potential for miscommunication and confusion.

Real-Time Insights and Analytics

In addition to its task management capabilities, the AI chatbot also provides valuable insights and analytics to help you make informed decisions. By analyzing the data it collects from team members and various project management tools, the chatbot can identify patterns, trends, and potential bottlenecks.

For example, it may detect that certain types of tasks consistently take longer than anticipated or that specific team members are repeatedly missing deadlines. With these insights, you can take corrective actions, such as adjusting timelines, providing additional training, or reallocating resources.

Continuous Learning and Improvement

One of the most significant advantages of the PMAI Method's Delegate and Track component is its ability to continuously learn and improve. As you and your team interact with the AI chatbot, it captures valuable data and feedback, which it can then use to refine its task delegation algorithms, communication strategies, and progress tracking methods.

Over time, the chatbot becomes more attuned to your team's dynamics, preferences, and working styles, allowing it to provide even more personalized and efficient support. This continuous learning loop ensures that the PMAI Method remains relevant and effective, even as your projects and team evolve.

In the fast-paced world of IT project management, the ability to delegate tasks effectively, monitor progress closely, and coordinate team efforts seamlessly can often mean the difference between success and failure. By embracing the Delegate and Track (D&T) component of the PMAI Method, you gain a powerful ally in the form of an AI chatbot assistant.

With its intelligent task allocation, real-time progress tracking, and streamlined communication capabilities, the chatbot empowers you to stay on top of your projects while freeing up valuable time and mental resources. As you continue to leverage this cutting-edge technology, you'll not only enhance your productivity but also position yourself as a forward-thinking leader in the IT project management landscape.

A Prompt for You To Try:

Prompt Name:	Task Delegation and Progress Tracking Assistant
Purpose:	Delegate tasks to team members and monitor progress.
Prompt:	Your task is to review the provided project plan and team member profiles, and intelligently assign tasks to the appropriate team members based on their skills, availability, and current workload. Once tasks are assigned, monitor the progress of each task and provide regular updates on the status, highlighting any potential delays or bottlenecks. Present the task assignments and progress updates in a clear and organized manner, using appropriate formatting such as a Kanban board or a spreadsheet.

6. REPORT AND COMMUNICATE VIA AI (R&C)

Keeping all project stakeholders informed and updated is crucial for success. However, gathering information from multiple sources and creating comprehensive reports can be tedious and time-consuming for project managers. This is where the Report and Communicate (R&C) element of the PMAI Method becomes invaluable, as it allows project managers to leverage the power of AI to streamline this process.

The R&C component focuses on using a text-based generative AI chatbot to automatically generate detailed status reports by aggregating data from various project sources. This capability saves significant time and effort for the project manager, while ensuring stakeholders remain well-informed throughout the project lifecycle.

THE PROCESS

Let's explore how the R&C process works in practice:

1. Data Collection

The first step involves gathering all the necessary project data that needs to be included in the status report. This could include information from project management tools like Jira or Microsoft Project, team collaboration platforms, meeting notes, and any other relevant documents or files.

2. Data Integration

Next, the project manager uploads or connects these data sources to the AI chatbot. The chatbot has the ability to integrate with a wide range of platforms and file formats, ensuring a seamless flow of information.

3. Report Generation

Once the data is accessible, the project manager can instruct the chatbot to generate a comprehensive status report. This can be done through a simple text prompt or by following pre-defined templates and preferences.

4. AI Analysis and Synthesis

The true power of the AI chatbot comes into play here. It analyzes the collected data, synthesizes the relevant information, and presents it in a cohesive and easily digestible format. The chatbot can highlight key milestones, identify potential risks or issues, and provide insights on project performance.

5. Customization and Review

While the AI-generated report provides a solid foundation, the project manager can further customize and fine-tune the content. This could involve adding additional commentary, adjusting the tone and language to suit the target audience, or incorporating specific project branding and visuals.

6. Distribution and Communication

With the final report ready, the project manager can distribute it to relevant stakeholders through various channels, such as email, project management tools, or shared document repositories. The AI chatbot can even assist in scheduling meetings or webinars to present and discuss the report findings.

BENEFITS OF THE R&C APPROACH

Adopting the R&C element of the PMAI Method offers several advantages for project managers:

1. Time Savings

One of the most significant benefits is the time saved by automating the report generation process. Project managers can reallocate this time to other critical tasks, such as strategic planning, risk mitigation, or team management.

2. Comprehensive and Consistent Reporting

By aggregating data from multiple sources, the AI chatbot ensures that status reports are comprehensive and consistent, reducing the risk of missing important information or providing conflicting updates.

3. Improved Communication and Transparency

Regular and informative status reports foster better communication and transparency with stakeholders. This helps build trust, manage expectations, and ensure everyone remains aligned with project goals and progress.

4. Data-driven Decision Making

The insights and analysis provided by the AI chatbot can support data-driven decision-making. Project managers can identify trends, anticipate potential issues, and make informed choices based on the synthesized information.

5. Scalability and Adaptability

As projects evolve or new data sources become available, the AI chatbot can easily adapt and incorporate the additional information into the reporting process, ensuring that reports remain comprehensive and up-to-date.

CONCLUSION

In today's fast-paced and data-driven project management landscape, the Report and Communicate (R&C) element of the PMAI Method offers a powerful solution for project managers. By leveraging the capabilities of a text-based generative AI chatbot, project managers can streamline the reporting process, improve communication and transparency with stakeholders, and make more informed decisions based on comprehensive and timely information.

Embracing this AI-enabled approach can significantly enhance project success and help project managers navigate the complexities of the modern IT industry.

A Prompt for You To Try:

Prompt Name:	Project Status Report Generator
Purpose:	Generate comprehensive project status reports by aggregating data from various sources.
Prompt:	Your task is to gather relevant project data from the provided sources (e.g., project management tools, team collaboration platforms, meeting notes, documents) and generate a comprehensive project status report. The report should include updates on progress, achieved milestones, identified risks or issues, and any necessary corrective actions. Present the report in a clear and organized manner, using appropriate formatting such as sections, headings, and visual aids (e.g., charts, graphs).

7. KNOWLEDGE AND STANDARDS CENTRALIZATION (K&S)

In today's fast-paced IT industry, project management is an ever-evolving field. With new technologies, methodologies, and best practices emerging rapidly, it's crucial for project managers to stay up-to-date and have access to the latest knowledge and standards. This is where the Knowledge and Standards Centralization (K&S) component of the PMAI Method comes into play.

The K&S component involves establishing the AI chatbot as a centralized repository for all project management-related knowledge and standards within an organization. By consolidating this information in one accessible location, project managers can quickly reference crucial resources, ensuring consistency and adherence to established guidelines.

Imagine having a virtual assistant that not only stores but also actively disseminates this valuable information. The chatbot becomes a hub for sharing and accessing best practices, lessons learned from previous projects, and the organization's specific standards and processes.

One of the key benefits of the K&S component is its ability to facilitate knowledge transfer and continuous learning. As new project managers join the team or existing members take on new roles, the chatbot can provide on-demand training and guidance, ensuring a smooth onboarding process and minimizing the learning curve.

For instance, a project manager overseeing a complex software development project could quickly access relevant methodologies, coding standards, and testing protocols stored within the chatbot's knowledge base. This not only ensures adherence to established guidelines but also promotes consistency across different project teams.

Furthermore, the K&S component can be especially valuable for organizations with geographically dispersed teams or those operating in a hybrid or remote work environment. By having a centralized source of information accessible from anywhere, project managers can ensure that all team members are aligned with the organization's standards, regardless of their physical location.

Beyond project-specific knowledge, the chatbot can also store and disseminate broader project management frameworks, such as Agile, Scrum, or Waterfall methodologies. This allows project managers to stay abreast of industry best practices and adapt their approach as needed, fostering an environment of continuous improvement and innovation.

Additionally, the K&S component can play a crucial role in risk management and compliance. By storing and referencing relevant industry regulations, security protocols, and organizational policies, project managers can proactively identify potential risks and ensure that their projects adhere to all necessary guidelines from the outset.

One of the key advantages of using an AI chatbot for knowledge and standards centralization is its ability to adapt and evolve. As new information or updates become available, the chatbot's knowledge base can be easily updated, ensuring that project managers always have access to the most current and relevant resources.

Moreover, the chatbot's natural language processing capabilities allow project managers to interact with the knowledge base in a more intuitive and conversational manner. Instead of sifting through lengthy documents or navigating complex databases, they can simply pose queries to the chatbot and receive concise, relevant responses tailored to their specific needs.

To further enhance the effectiveness of the K&S component, the chatbot can be integrated with other project management tools and platforms. For example, it could be linked to document management systems, allowing project managers to seamlessly access and reference relevant files and resources directly from within the chatbot interface.

In summary, the Knowledge and Standards Centralization (K&S) component of the PMAI Method provides project managers with a powerful tool for consolidating and disseminating crucial knowledge and standards.

By establishing the AI chatbot as a centralized repository, project managers can access and share best practices, lessons learned, and organizational guidelines with ease. This not only promotes consistency and adherence to established standards but also fosters an environment of continuous learning and improvement, ultimately contributing to the success of projects and the overall growth of the organization.

A Prompt for You To Try:

Prompt Name:	Project Knowledge Base Assistant
Purpose:	Consolidate and disseminate project management knowledge and standards.
Prompt:	Your task is to create a centralized knowledge base for project management best practices, lessons learned, organizational standards, and relevant industry guidelines. The knowledge base should be organized and structured in a way that allows for easy access and retrieval of information. Incorporate any provided materials, such as process documentation, case studies, or training resources, and present the information in a clear and user-friendly manner.

8. Allocate and Optimize Resources (A&O)

Effective resource allocation and optimization are critical components of successful project management. By leveraging the capabilities of an AI chatbot, project managers can significantly enhance their ability to assign and manage resources efficiently. The Allocate and Optimize (A&O) element of the PMAI Method provides a structured approach to achieving this goal.

At the core of the A&O process is the analysis of project requirements against available resources. This involves a comprehensive assessment of the skills, expertise, and capacities required for each project task, as well as an inventory of the resources at the project manager's disposal. These resources may include team members with varying skill sets, equipment, software tools, and budget allocations.

The AI chatbot plays a pivotal role in this analysis by collating and processing data from multiple sources. It can integrate information from project plans, team member profiles, resource management systems, and historical project data. By applying advanced analytical algorithms, the chatbot can identify potential resource constraints, skill gaps, and capacity limitations that may impact the project's successful execution.

Once the analysis is complete, the chatbot can provide recommendations for optimal resource allocation. This may involve suggesting the most suitable team members for specific tasks based on their expertise and availability. It can also propose alternative resource configurations or suggest the acquisition of additional resources if necessary.

For example, if the project requires specialized expertise in a particular programming language or technology, the chatbot can identify team members with the relevant skills or recommend bringing in external consultants or contractors. Similarly, if there is a shortage of hardware resources, such as servers or workstations, the chatbot can suggest leasing or cloud-based solutions to meet the project's requirements.

Furthermore, the chatbot can assist in monitoring and adjusting resource allocation throughout the project lifecycle. As tasks are completed and new requirements emerge, the chatbot can dynamically update resource assignments, ensuring that resources are utilized optimally and not left idle or overburdened.

One of the key benefits of the A&O element is its ability to identify and mitigate potential resource conflicts or bottlenecks. By analyzing resource dependencies and forecasting future demand, the chatbot can alert project managers to potential resource clashes or capacity constraints well in advance. This allows for proactive planning and mitigation strategies, such as reallocating resources, staggering task schedules, or acquiring additional resources.

The A&O element also supports cost optimization by recommending the most cost-effective resource configurations. The chatbot can analyze the budget constraints and suggest ways to achieve the desired project outcomes while minimizing expenses. This may involve leveraging existing in-house resources, negotiating better rates with vendors, or exploring alternative solutions that deliver equivalent results at a lower cost.

In addition to resource allocation and optimization, the chatbot can assist with ongoing resource management tasks. These may include tracking resource utilization, generating resource utilization reports, and providing insights into resource performance and productivity. This data can inform future resource planning and optimization efforts, contributing to a continuous cycle of improvement.

To illustrate the A&O element in action, consider a project involving the development of a new mobile application for a retail company. The project manager could use the AI chatbot to analyze the project requirements, such as the desired features, target platforms, and deadlines. The chatbot would then assess the available resources, including the company's in-house development team, external contractors, software tools, and hardware infrastructure.

Based on this analysis, the chatbot might recommend allocating specific developers to work on different components of the app based on their expertise and availability. It could also suggest outsourcing certain tasks, such as user interface design or testing, to external contractors or freelancers to ensure timely delivery. **Additionally**, the chatbot might identify the need for additional server capacity to support the app's deployment and recommend cloud-based solutions as a cost-effective option.

Throughout the project's lifecycle, the chatbot would continuously monitor resource utilization and provide insights into potential bottlenecks or capacity constraints. If unexpected issues or changes in requirements arise, the chatbot could suggest adjustments to resource allocation, such as temporarily reassigning team members or bringing in additional resources to meet the revised project timelines.

By leveraging the A&O element of the PMAI Method and the capabilities of an AI chatbot, project managers can make informed decisions about resource allocation, optimize resource utilization, and mitigate potential risks associated with resource constraints.

This proactive approach to resource management increases the likelihood of delivering projects successfully, on time, and within budget, while also contributing to the overall efficiency and productivity of the organization.

A Prompt for You To Try:

Prompt Name:	Resource Allocation and Optimization Assistant
Purpose:	Analyze project requirements and optimize resource allocation.
Prompt:	Your task is to review the provided project requirements, including desired features, target platforms, deadlines, and budget constraints, and analyze the available resources (e.g., development team, external contractors, software tools, hardware infrastructure). Based on this analysis, provide recommendations for optimal resource allocation, including suggestions for outsourcing or acquiring additional resources if necessary. Present the resource allocation recommendations in a clear and organized manner, considering factors such as cost-effectiveness, skill matching, and resource utilization.

9. TRAIN AND ONBOARD WITH AI ASSISTANCE (T&O)

In today's fast-paced IT industry, project teams are often assembled quickly. New members may join mid-project or take on roles they have limited experience with. Ramping up these individuals efficiently is crucial to keeping projects on track. The Train and Onboard (T&O) component of the PMAI Method leverages an AI assistant to streamline team training and onboarding processes.

The AI assistant acts as an ever-present guide, providing on-demand access to customized project information and training materials. This allows new team members to get up to speed rapidly without overloading experienced staff with excessive questions or guidance requests.

Getting Started with Project Fundamentals

When a new member joins a project, their AI assistant can provide a comprehensive overview tailored to their specific role. This covers key details like:

- Project background and objectives
- Responsibilities of their role
- Stakeholder information
- Methodologies and processes used
- Access to project documentation

The AI assistant distills volumes of information into concise, relevant summaries. New members can quickly understand the project context without wading through excessive documentation.

For instance, Sara recently joined a team developing a cloud-based HR application. Her AI assistant provided a rundown of the project's goals, technologies used, sprint cadences, and relevant UX design standards. This allowed Sara to immediately start contributing rather than spending days reviewing materials.

On-Demand Learning and Support

As new situations arise, the AI assistant enables just-in-time learning opportunities. Team members can ask questions using natural language and receive explanations at an appropriate level.

For example, a junior developer named Amir asked his AI assistant to explain the coding standards used for the front-end components he was working on. The assistant provided a clear overview, examples, and highlighted relevant documentation sections for Amir to reference.

The AI assistant also tracks areas where team members need additional support. It can proactively suggest training materials or facilitate conversations with subject matter experts when knowledge gaps are identified.

Reinforcing Organizational Processes

Project management processes and compliance requirements are also an area where the AI assistant provides significant value during onboarding.

The assistant acts as a universal source encompassing an organization's full set of processes, standards, and policy documentation. It can guide new team members through implementing processes like code reviews, test plans, risk logs, and audit activities correctly from day one.

For an IT firm adopting DevOps practices, the AI assistant ensures all new engineers follow defined continuous integration and deployment processes flawlessly. This elevates consistency and minimizes costly errors caused by deviance from approved methods.

Facilitating Knowledge Sharing

Beyond codified processes, the AI assistant captures insights from experienced team members. This tribal knowledge is often undocumented but essential for working effectively.

For instance, veteran developers can share techniques for optimizing code performance on the company's cloud platform. Designers can provide nuanced guidelines on applying the latest UX patterns. These invaluable tips get incorporated into the AI's knowledge base.

New team members can query for and assimilate this hands-on

guidance naturally through conversations with the AI assistant. The barrier to accessing insights from colleagues is lowered significantly.

Continuously Updating and Refining

As the project evolves, having an AI assistant enables continuous learning. Lessons, new processes, updated artifacts, and fresh knowledge get seamlessly integrated into the assistant's corpus.

If UX design standards change during an application's development, the AI assistant is promptly updated. It immediately begins coaching team members on the new guidelines. This fosters rapid dissemination of changes across the team, reducing inconsistencies and rework.

Developers exploring implementation options can leverage the AI assistant as a research tool. The assistant digests and synthesizes technical documentation to provide focused, actionable recommendations tuned to the project's needs.

For project managers themselves, the AI assistant acts as an experienced virtual mentor. The assistant offers advice on leadership approaches, situational handling, and alignment with organizational practices, cultivating continuous professional development.

Maximizing Efficiency and Consistency

Through the Train and Onboard (T&O) use case, the PMAI Method enables effortlessly ramping up new team members. The AI assistant eliminates knowledge silos, allowing insights to flow freely across projects.

Team members gain autonomy in acquiring knowledge when needed through intuitive natural language interactions. This reduces overwhelming experienced staff with basic queries, maximizing their focus on high-value tasks.

Overall, the PMAI Method's T&O component drives greater team productivity and consistency in execution. By facilitating dynamic learning, it empowers projects to rapidly capitalize on new opportunities through the collective knowledge of the entire organization.

A Prompt for You To Try:

Prompt Name:	Team Onboarding and Training Assistant
Purpose:	Streamline team training and onboarding processes.
Prompt:	Your task is to create a tailored onboarding and training program for new team members joining the project. The program should include an overview of the project background, objectives, methodologies, and processes, as well as specific information and resources relevant to the individual's role. Additionally, provide guidance on organizational processes, compliance requirements, and best practices. Present the onboarding and training materials in a clear and organized manner, using appropriate formatting and interactive components.

10. GENERATE AND REFINE PROJECT CONTENT (G&R)

Creating high-quality project documentation is crucial for effective project management. However, it can be a time-consuming and challenging task, especially when dealing with complex projects. That's where the Generate and Refine (G&R) component of the PMAI

Method comes into play. By leveraging the power of a text-based generative AI chatbot, project managers can streamline the content creation process while maintaining a professional standard.

The G&R component is designed to assist project managers in two key areas: generating initial drafts of project-related content and refining those drafts to meet the required quality and formatting standards. Let's explore how this component works and the benefits it provides.

Generating Initial Drafts

The first step in the G&R process is to generate an initial draft of the project content you need. This could include project proposals, status reports, presentations, or any other documentation required throughout the project lifecycle.

To initiate the draft generation process, you simply need to provide the AI chatbot with the necessary information and context. This could include details about the project scope, objectives, stakeholders, timelines, and any specific requirements or guidelines.

For example, let's say you need to create a project proposal for a new IT initiative. You could provide the chatbot with information such as the project's background, goals, deliverables, budget estimates, and any other relevant details. The chatbot would then use this information to generate a draft proposal, complete with sections like executive summary, project description, approach, timeline, and budget.

The beauty of using an AI chatbot for this task is that it can save you a significant amount of time and effort. Instead of starting from scratch, you have a solid foundation to build upon, allowing you to focus your efforts on reviewing and refining the content.

Refining the Content

Once you have an initial draft, the next step is to refine the content to ensure it meets your organization's standards and aligns with the specific project requirements. This is where the true power of the G&R component comes into play.

The AI chatbot can assist you in several ways during the refinement process:

1. **Formatting and Style Consistency:** The chatbot can help ensure that the content adheres to your organization's formatting guidelines, including font styles, headings, and layout.

2. **Language and Tone:** The chatbot can analyze the language used in the draft and suggest improvements to ensure clarity, conciseness, and alignment with the desired tone and voice.

3. **Incorporating Feedback:** If you receive feedback or additional input from stakeholders, you can provide that information to the chatbot, which can then incorporate the changes into the draft.

4. **Customization:** The chatbot can help you tailor the content to specific audiences or stakeholders by suggesting language or formatting changes based on their preferences or requirements.

5. **Fact-checking and Research:** If you need to verify information or conduct additional research, the chatbot can assist in finding and integrating relevant data or sources into the content.

Throughout the refinement process, you maintain control over the final product. The chatbot acts as an intelligent assistant, providing suggestions and recommendations based on the information and feedback you provide. You can choose to accept, modify, or reject any proposed changes, ensuring that the final content meets your exact specifications.

Benefits of the G&R Component

Incorporating the Generate and Refine (G&R) component into your project management workflow offers several key benefits:

1. **Time Savings:** By automating the initial content generation and providing intelligent assistance during the refinement process, the G&R component can significantly reduce the time and effort required to create high-quality project documentation.

2. **Consistency and Quality:** The chatbot's ability to adhere to formatting guidelines and language standards helps ensure consistency across all project documentation, while its analytical capabilities help maintain a high level of quality.

3. **Collaboration and Feedback Integration:** The seamless integration of feedback and input from stakeholders streamlines the collaboration process, ensuring that all perspectives are considered and incorporated into the final content.

4. **Knowledge Retention:** By leveraging the chatbot's knowledge base, you can capture and retain project-specific information and learnings, facilitating knowledge transfer and continuous improvement across future projects.

5. **Scalability:** As your project documentation needs grow, the G&R component can scale to meet those demands, providing a consistent and efficient approach to content creation and refinement.

By embracing the **Generate and Refine (G&R)** component of the PMAI Method, project managers can unlock new levels of productivity and efficiency in their content creation processes.

With the assistance of a text-based generative AI chatbot, you can focus your efforts on strategic decision-making and project oversight while ensuring that your documentation meets the highest standards of quality and professionalism.

A Prompt for You To Try:

Prompt Name:	Project Content Creation and Refinement Assistant
Purpose:	Generate initial drafts and refine project-related content.
Prompt:	Your task is to assist in creating and refining project-related content, such as proposals, reports, presentations, or any other documentation. Provide a clear description of the content required, including the intended audience, purpose, and any specific guidelines or requirements. You can then generate an initial draft based on the provided information, which I will review and refine. Throughout the refinement process, assist with formatting, language improvements, incorporating feedback, and ensuring adherence to organizational standards.

To better understand how the PMAI Method leverages AI chatbots, we invite you to interact with our ProjectPal GPT.

Visit: www.rethinkprojectmanagement.com

4

OVERCOMING OBJECTIONS TO AI ADOPTION

ADDRESSING DOUBTS ABOUT AI RELIABILITY

One of the primary concerns project managers may have about adopting a text-based generative AI chatbot is the reliability of the technology itself. After all, these tools are still relatively new, and the idea of relying on an AI for critical project tasks can seem daunting.

It's essential to understand that modern AI systems, particularly those developed by reputable companies like Anthropic, are built on robust foundations of machine learning and natural language processing. These systems are trained on vast amounts of data, allowing them to develop a comprehensive understanding of language, context, and problem-solving.

However, it's important to recognize that no AI system is perfect, and there may be instances where the chatbot's responses are inaccurate or require additional human oversight. This is where the human-AI collaboration aspect of the PMAI method comes into play.

By leveraging the chatbot's capabilities as a supportive tool rather than a complete replacement for human expertise, project managers can harness the AI's strengths while maintaining control over critical decision-making processes. The chatbot can handle time-consuming tasks like document analysis, meeting summaries, and risk identification, freeing up the project manager's time for strategic thinking and decision-making.

Furthermore, it's crucial to understand that the chatbot's responses are based on the quality of the data it was trained on and the specific prompts provided by the user. By carefully crafting prompts and providing high-quality project documentation, project managers can significantly improve the accuracy and usefulness of the chatbot's outputs.

To address doubts about reliability, project managers should start by testing the chatbot on low-risk tasks and gradually increase its involvement as they gain confidence in its capabilities. Regular monitoring and validation of the chatbot's outputs are also essential to ensure that it is performing as expected.

Additionally, it's important to remember that AI technology is rapidly evolving, and chatbots are becoming increasingly sophisticated and reliable over time. By embracing this technology early on, project managers can stay ahead of the curve and develop a competitive advantage in their field.

OVERCOMING RESISTANCE TO AI IN PROJECT MANAGEMENT

The adoption of new technologies often faces resistance, and the integration of AI in project management is no exception. Some project managers may be hesitant to embrace AI tools, fearing that they will disrupt established workflows or render their expertise obsolete.

However, it's important to recognize that AI is not a replacement for human project managers but rather a powerful tool to augment their capabilities. The PMAI method is designed to leverage the strengths of both human and AI, creating a synergistic partnership that enhances productivity and project success.

One of the key advantages of AI in project management is its ability to handle repetitive, time-consuming tasks with accuracy and efficiency. By offloading tasks like document analysis, meeting summaries, and progress tracking to the AI chatbot, project managers can free up valuable time and mental resources to focus on higher-level strategic thinking, decision-making, and team leadership.

Furthermore, the AI chatbot can provide valuable insights and recommendations based on its analysis of project data, identifying potential risks and opportunities that may be overlooked by human project managers. This can lead to more informed decision-making and better overall project outcomes.

To overcome resistance to AI adoption, it's crucial to educate project managers and teams about the benefits and limitations of the technology. Highlighting successful case studies and providing hands-on training can help demystify AI and demonstrate its practical applications in project management.

Additionally, addressing concerns about job security is essential. Project managers should be reassured that the AI chatbot is not intended to replace them but rather to enhance their productivity and effectiveness. By embracing AI as a collaborative partner, project managers can future-proof their careers and remain competitive in an increasingly technology-driven industry.

Ultimately, the adoption of AI in project management is an opportunity to streamline processes, improve decision-making, and drive better project outcomes. By overcoming initial resistance and embracing the PMAI method, project managers can position themselves as leaders in their field and stay ahead of the curve in an ever-evolving technological landscape.

AI WON'T REPLACE HUMAN PROJECT MANAGERS

One of the most common concerns about adopting a text-based generative AI chatbot in project management is the fear that it could eventually replace human project managers altogether. However, this fear is largely unfounded, as AI is designed to augment and support human capabilities rather than replace them entirely.

While AI chatbots can excel at specific tasks like data analysis, document summarization, and task delegation, they lack the critical thinking, emotional intelligence, and strategic decision-making skills that are essential for effective project management. Projects often involve complex stakeholder relationships, dynamic environments, and unforeseen challenges that require human judgment, empathy, and adaptability.

The PMAI method recognizes this limitation and positions the AI chatbot as a collaborative tool to assist project managers rather than a replacement. By offloading repetitive and time-consuming tasks to the chatbot, project managers can focus their efforts on the more strategic and human-centric aspects of project management, such as team leadership, risk mitigation, and stakeholder management.

Furthermore, the PMAI method acknowledges that the human project manager remains the ultimate decision-maker, responsible for reviewing and validating the chatbot's outputs and ensuring that they align with project objectives and stakeholder needs. The chatbot serves as a valuable resource and advisor, but it does not have the authority to make critical project decisions independently.

It's also important to recognize that project management is a multifaceted discipline that requires a diverse set of skills beyond just technical expertise. Effective project managers must possess strong communication, negotiation, and conflict resolution abilities, as well as the ability to inspire and motivate team members. These "soft skills" are inherently human traits that AI has yet to replicate effectively.

As AI technology continues to evolve, it is likely that chatbots will become even more sophisticated and capable of handling more complex tasks. However, it is highly improbable that AI will ever completely replace the need for human project managers. Instead, the future of project management lies in a harmonious collaboration between human and AI capabilities, where the strengths of each are leveraged to achieve optimal project outcomes.

By embracing the PMAI method and viewing the AI chatbot as a supportive tool rather than a threat, project managers can alleviate concerns about job replacement and focus on enhancing their productivity, decision-making, and overall effectiveness in managing projects.

DEBUNKING MYTHS ABOUT AI COMPLEXITY AND COST

One of the common misconceptions about adopting a text-based generative AI chatbot for project management is the perception that it is a complex and costly undertaking. However, this is largely a myth, and the PMAI method aims to simplify and democratize the integration of AI into project management processes.

Firstly, it's important to understand that modern AI chatbots are designed to be user-friendly and accessible, even for those without extensive technical expertise. The PMAI method leverages these chatbots as intuitive tools that can be easily integrated into existing project management workflows without the need for complex coding or programming skills.

Contrary to popular belief, adopting an AI chatbot does not necessarily require a significant upfront investment or costly infrastructure. Many reputable AI companies offer affordable subscription-based pricing models or pay-as-you-go plans, making it accessible for organizations of various sizes and budgets.

Furthermore, the long-term benefits of adopting an AI chatbot can far outweigh the initial costs. By streamlining processes, improving decision-making, and enhancing team productivity, the PMAI method can lead to significant time and cost savings, ultimately contributing to the overall profitability and competitiveness of the organization.

Another myth surrounding AI adoption is the perception that it requires extensive training and specialized expertise. While some basic training and familiarization may be necessary, the PMAI method is designed to be intuitive and user-friendly, with the chatbot acting as a collaborative partner that can learn and adapt to the project manager's specific needs and workflows over time.

It's also important to note that the PMAI method advocates for a gradual and iterative approach to AI adoption. Project managers can start by incorporating the chatbot into low-risk tasks and gradually increase its involvement as they gain confidence in its capabilities. This incremental approach minimizes disruption and allows for a smooth transition, alleviating concerns about complexity and reducing the perceived risk.

By debunking these myths and highlighting the accessibility and potential benefits of the PMAI method, project managers can approach AI adoption with confidence, recognizing it as a valuable tool for enhancing their productivity and project success

In addition to addressing the perceived complexity and cost barriers, it's also important to debunk the myth that adopting AI requires a complete overhaul of existing systems and processes. The PMAI method is designed to be flexible and adaptable, allowing project managers to seamlessly integrate the AI chatbot into their current workflows without the need for significant disruptions or changes.

By starting small and gradually incorporating the chatbot into specific tasks or phases of the project management process, project managers can mitigate the perceived risks and complexity associated with AI adoption. The PMAI method provides a structured approach to leveraging the chatbot's capabilities, ensuring a smooth transition and minimizing the potential for errors or disruptions.

Overall, by dispelling the myths surrounding AI complexity and cost, project managers can approach the adoption of a text-based generative AI chatbot with an open and informed mindset, recognizing it as an accessible and potentially game-changing tool for enhancing their productivity and project success.

ALLEVIATING FEARS ABOUT AI ERRORS AND BIASES

Another common concern among project managers when considering the adoption of a text-based generative AI chatbot is the potential for errors and biases in the AI's outputs. While this is a valid concern, it's important to recognize that the PMAI method is designed to address these issues and provide a robust framework for mitigating risks.

Firstly, it's essential to understand that AI systems, like any tool, are not infallible and may produce errors or biased outputs if not used correctly or if the underlying data is flawed. However, by following best practices and implementing appropriate safeguards, project managers can significantly reduce the likelihood of such occurrences.

One of the key strategies employed by the PMAI method is the emphasis on human oversight and validation. The AI chatbot is positioned as a supportive tool, providing recommendations and insights, but the ultimate decision-making authority rests with the human project manager. By carefully reviewing and validating the chatbot's outputs, project managers can identify and correct any potential errors or biases before they impact project outcomes.

Additionally, the PMAI method advocates for ongoing monitoring and fine-tuning of the chatbot's performance. Regular evaluation and feedback loops can help identify areas where the chatbot may be underperforming or exhibiting biases, allowing for adjustments to be made to the underlying data or algorithms.

To alleviate fears about AI errors and biases, project managers should also prioritize transparency and explainability in the AI's decision-making processes. By understanding how the chatbot arrives at its recommendations and the factors it considers, project managers can better assess the validity and reliability of the outputs.

Furthermore, the PMAI method encourages the use of diverse data sources and perspectives when training the AI chatbot. By exposing the chatbot to a wide range of information and viewpoints, the risk of perpetuating biases or forming narrow perspectives is significantly reduced.

It's also important to note that the AI chatbot is not a black box; it is a tool that can be continuously improved and refined through ongoing training and feedback. As the field of AI ethics and bias mitigation continues to evolve, project managers can benefit from adopting industry best practices and staying informed about the latest developments.

By implementing these strategies and acknowledging the potential for errors and biases while taking proactive measures to mitigate them, project managers can alleviate their concerns and leverage the power of AI chatbots with confidence, while maintaining a commitment to ethical and responsible AI adoption.

BALANCING HUMAN-AI COLLABORATION CHALLENGES

While the PMAI method promotes the seamless integration of a text-based generative AI chatbot into project management workflows, it's important to acknowledge and address the potential challenges that may arise in the human-AI collaboration process.

One of the primary challenges is striking the right balance between leveraging the AI's capabilities and maintaining human control and oversight. Project managers may initially struggle with determining which tasks to delegate to the chatbot and which ones require direct human involvement. This can lead to either an over-reliance on the AI or an underutilization of its potential.

To address this challenge, the PMAI method provides a structured framework that helps project managers identify the most suitable tasks for AI assistance.

By clearly defining the roles and responsibilities of both the human and the AI, project managers can establish clear boundaries and ensure that the chatbot is used effectively without compromising critical decision-making processes.

Another potential challenge is the communication barrier that may arise between humans and AI systems. While modern chatbots are designed to understand and communicate in natural language, there may still be instances where the AI misinterprets instructions or provides responses that are unclear or lacking context.

To mitigate this challenge, the PMAI method emphasizes the importance of clear and concise prompting when interacting with the chatbot. Project managers should be trained in effective prompt engineering techniques to ensure that their instructions and queries are unambiguous and tailored to the chatbot's capabilities.

Additionally, the PMAI method encourages regular feedback loops and iterative refinement of the chatbot's responses. By providing constructive feedback and engaging in a collaborative learning process, project managers can help the chatbot adapt and improve its communication over time, fostering a more seamless human-AI collaboration experience.

Another potential challenge is the acceptance and trust of the AI chatbot by project team members and stakeholders. Some individuals may be skeptical of relying on AI-generated outputs or recommendations, particularly in critical project decisions.

To address this challenge, the PMAI method advocates for transparency and open communication about the AI chatbot's role and limitations. By educating team members and stakeholders on the underlying principles of the PMAI method and the safeguards in place, project managers can build trust and ensure that the AI chatbot is perceived as a valuable asset rather than a source of concern.

By acknowledging and proactively addressing these human-AI collaboration challenges, project managers can navigate the transition to AI-assisted project management with confidence and ensure that the benefits of the PMAI method are fully realized.

STARTING SMALL: PRACTICAL FIRST STEPS WITH AI

One of the most effective ways to overcome objections and concerns about adopting a text-based generative AI chatbot for project management is to start small and take practical, incremental steps. The PMAI method is designed to facilitate a gradual integration of AI into existing project management workflows, allowing project managers to build confidence and experience with the technology at their own pace.

The first step in this journey is to identify low-risk, repetitive tasks that can be delegated to the AI chatbot. These tasks could include meeting note summarization, document analysis, or progress tracking. By starting with these relatively simple tasks, project managers can gain hands-on experience with the chatbot's capabilities and observe its performance in a controlled environment.

As project managers become more comfortable with the chatbot's outputs and develop a better understanding of its strengths and limitations, they can gradually expand its involvement to more complex tasks, such as risk identification, resource allocation, or content generation.

It's important to note that the PMAI method is not a one-size-fits-all solution, and project managers should tailor their approach based on their specific needs, project requirements, and team dynamics. The iterative nature of the method allows for continuous learning and adaptation, ensuring that the AI chatbot is integrated seamlessly into the project management process.

To facilitate a smooth transition, project managers should consider conducting small-scale pilot projects or simulations before implementing the PMAI method on larger, more critical projects. This approach not only provides valuable training opportunities but also helps identify potential roadblocks or areas for improvement before committing significant resources.

Throughout the implementation process, it's essential to maintain open communication with team members and stakeholders. Sharing successes, challenges, and lessons learned can help build trust and acceptance of the AI chatbot, while also fostering an environment of continuous learning and improvement.

By starting small and taking practical first steps, project managers can alleviate concerns about the complexity or risk associated with AI adoption. They can gradually build their confidence and expertise, while also demonstrating the tangible benefits of the PMAI method to their teams and stakeholders.

BUILDING SELF-BELIEF AND EVALUATING ROI

Adopting a new technology like a text-based generative AI chatbot for project management can be a significant undertaking, and it's natural for project managers to have doubts or concerns about their ability to implement the PMAI method successfully. Building self-belief and evaluating the potential return on investment (ROI) are crucial steps in overcoming these objections.

One of the key strategies for building self-belief is to focus on the tangible benefits and success stories of AI adoption in project management. By researching case studies and real-world examples of how the PMAI method or similar AI-assisted approaches have improved project outcomes, increased productivity, and enhanced decision-making, project managers can gain confidence in the potential of this technology.

Additionally, it's important to recognize that the PMAI method is designed to be a collaborative partnership between human and AI. The chatbot is not meant to replace the project manager's expertise but rather to augment and support their capabilities. By embracing this mindset, project managers can view the AI as a valuable tool in their arsenal, empowering them to achieve even greater success in their roles.

To build self-belief, it's also essential to start small and celebrate incremental successes. By gradually incorporating the AI chatbot into low-risk tasks and witnessing its positive impact firsthand, project managers can gain confidence in their ability to leverage this technology effectively. Each successful implementation, no matter how small, can serve as a stepping stone towards embracing more advanced applications of the PMAI method.

Another effective strategy for building self-belief is to seek out training and support resources. Participating in workshops, webinars, or online communities focused on AI adoption in project management can provide valuable insights, best practices, and opportunities to learn from experienced professionals. This continuous learning process not only enhances knowledge but also reinforces a growth mindset, which is crucial for embracing new technologies.

In addition to building self-belief, it's important for project managers to evaluate the potential return on investment (ROI) of adopting the PMAI method. While there may be upfront costs associated with acquiring an AI chatbot and implementing the necessary infrastructure, the long-term benefits can be substantial.

By leveraging the chatbot's capabilities to streamline processes, automate repetitive tasks, and enhance decision-making, project managers can realize significant time and cost savings. These efficiencies can translate into improved project delivery times, reduced operational costs, and increased productivity for team members.

Furthermore, the PMAI method can contribute to better project outcomes by reducing the risk of errors, identifying potential issues early on, and optimizing resource allocation. This can lead to higher customer satisfaction, stronger stakeholder relationships, and a competitive advantage for the organization.

To evaluate ROI effectively, project managers should establish clear metrics and Key Performance Indicators (KPIs) aligned with their organizational goals. These could include measures such as project delivery times, cost savings, resource utilization, customer satisfaction scores, or overall project success rates.

By tracking these metrics before and after implementing the PMAI method, project managers can quantify the real-world impact of adopting the AI chatbot and demonstrate its value to stakeholders and decision-makers within the organization.

Ultimately, building self-belief and evaluating the potential ROI are crucial steps in overcoming objections to AI adoption in project management. By focusing on tangible benefits, celebrating successes, seeking support, and measuring the impact, project managers can confidently embrace the PMAI method as a powerful tool for enhancing their capabilities and driving project success.

WHEN IS THE RIGHT TIME TO ADOPT AI?

Deciding when to adopt a text-based generative AI chatbot for project management is a common concern for many professionals.

While the benefits of the PMAI method are compelling, project managers may wonder if there is an ideal time or set of circumstances that make the transition to AI-assisted project management more advantageous.

The truth is, there is no one-size-fits-all answer, as the right time to adopt AI will vary depending on the specific needs, goals, and readiness of each project manager and their organization. However, there are several factors that can help guide this decision and ensure a smoother transition.

One key consideration is the current workload and complexity of projects being managed. If project managers find themselves consistently overwhelmed by the volume of tasks, documentation, and communication required, it may be an opportune time to explore the PMAI method. The AI chatbot can alleviate some of these burdens by streamlining processes, automating repetitive tasks, and providing valuable insights and recommendations.

Additionally, if an organization is facing increased competition or market pressures that demand faster project delivery, improved efficiency, and enhanced decision-making capabilities, adopting the PMAI method can provide a competitive edge. By leveraging the AI chatbot's capabilities, project managers can optimize resource allocation, identify potential risks and opportunities more effectively, and ultimately deliver projects with greater success.

Another factor to consider is the organization's readiness for digital transformation and the adoption of new technologies. If there is already a culture of innovation and a willingness to embrace emerging tools and methodologies, the transition to AI-assisted project management may be more seamless. Conversely, if there is significant resistance to change or a lack of understanding about AI, it may be beneficial to invest in education and change management efforts before implementing the PMAI method.

It's also important to assess the availability of resources and support for AI adoption within the organization. If there is dedicated budget, infrastructure, and expertise to facilitate the implementation of the PMAI method, the timing may be more favorable. Conversely, if resources are limited or there is a lack of technical support, it may be prudent to address these gaps before proceeding with AI adoption.

Ultimately, the right time to adopt the PMAI method is when the potential benefits outweigh the perceived risks and challenges, and when the organization is ready to embrace the change. Project managers should carefully evaluate their current situation, organizational goals, and readiness factors to determine the most opportune moment for integrating a text-based generative AI chatbot into their project management practices.

MANAGING TIME AND BUDGET FOR AI IMPLEMENTATION

One of the common objections to adopting a text-based generative AI chatbot for project management is the perceived time and budget requirements associated with the implementation process. While it's true that integrating new technology can demand resources, the PMAI method is designed to be cost-effective and time-efficient, making AI adoption accessible to organizations of various sizes and budgets.

Time Management:

Effective time management is crucial when implementing the PMAI method. Project managers should begin by allocating dedicated time for training and familiarization with the AI chatbot. This initial investment of time will pay dividends in the long run, as it will ensure that the team is proficient in utilizing the chatbot's capabilities effectively.

Additionally, it's important to recognize that the PMAI method is not a one-time implementation but rather an iterative process. Project managers should plan for regular check-ins and adjustments to the chatbot's performance, as well as ongoing training and knowledge sharing among team members.

To streamline the implementation process, the PMAI method recommends starting small by identifying low-risk, repetitive tasks that can be delegated to the chatbot. This approach not only minimizes disruptions to ongoing projects but also allows for a gradual learning curve and adaptation to the new technology.

As the team becomes more comfortable with the chatbot's capabilities, additional tasks and responsibilities can be gradually integrated into the AI-assisted workflow. This incremental approach ensures that the transition is smooth and manageable within the project manager's existing time constraints.

Budget Considerations:

Regarding budget considerations, the PMAI method acknowledges that the initial investment in an AI chatbot may be a concern for some organizations. However, it's important to weigh the upfront costs against the long-term benefits and potential return on investment (ROI).

Many reputable AI companies offer flexible pricing models, such as subscription-based plans or pay-as-you-go options, making the technology more accessible to organizations of various sizes and budgets. Project managers should carefully evaluate the costs associated with different chatbot solutions and select the one that best aligns with their needs and financial constraints.

Additionally, it's essential to consider the potential cost savings and efficiencies that can be achieved through the implementation of the PMAI method. By automating repetitive tasks, streamlining processes, and enhancing decision-making, the chatbot can contribute to significant time and resource savings, ultimately offsetting the initial investment costs.

To effectively manage the budget for AI implementation, project managers should create a detailed plan that accounts for not only the chatbot acquisition costs but also any necessary infrastructure upgrades, training expenses, and ongoing maintenance and support requirements.

By carefully allocating resources and prioritizing the most critical tasks for AI assistance, project managers can maximize the return on investment while minimizing unnecessary expenditures.

Ultimately, by adopting a strategic and proactive approach to time and budget management, project managers can overcome objections and successfully implement the PMAI method, unlocking the transformative potential of AI-assisted project management without compromising their existing workflows or financial constraints.

Before embarking on your AI adoption journey, it's essential to understand your organization's unique challenges and requirements. Take our free assessment at: www.rethinkprojectmanagement.com/assessment to identify areas where AI can provide the most value.

5

IMPLEMENTING THE PMAI METHOD

The Project Management AI Integration (PMAI) Method offers an exciting opportunity to revolutionize how we approach project management. By leveraging the capabilities of text-based generative AI chatbots, project managers can unlock unprecedented levels of productivity, efficiency, and project success.

As we've explored, the current landscape for IT project managers is rife with challenges, from rapid technological advancements to increased complexity, remote work environments, cybersecurity concerns, and budgetary constraints. Navigating these obstacles while striving for successful project delivery, career growth, and strategic impact can be overwhelming.

Fortunately, the PMAI Method provides a structured approach to harness the power of AI chatbots, transforming the way we plan, execute, and manage projects. By integrating AI into our workflows, we can overcome doubts, alleviate workloads, and unlock productivity like never before.

ENCOURAGING ENGAGEMENT WITH TEXT-BASED GENERATIVE AI CHATBOTS

The first step towards implementing the PMAI Method is to embrace the potential of text-based generative AI chatbots. While these chatbots may seem like a novel concept, they are quickly becoming an indispensable tool for professionals across various industries, including project management.

One of the key advantages of using AI chatbots is their ability to process and synthesize vast amounts of information quickly and accurately. This capability is invaluable in the project management realm, where data analysis and decision-making are critical components of success.

Furthermore, AI chatbots can streamline and automate many routine tasks, freeing up valuable time for project managers to focus on higher-level strategic thinking and problem-solving. From meeting summarization to task delegation and progress tracking, these chatbots can simplify and enhance the entire project management process.

To encourage engagement with text-based generative AI chatbots, it's essential to educate yourself and your team on their potential benefits. Attend workshops, webinars, or read case studies highlighting successful implementations of AI chatbots in project management. This knowledge will help alleviate any doubts or hesitations and foster a culture of innovation within your organization.

The first step in implementing the PMAI Method is to assess your organization's current project management processes and pain points. Our free online assessment at: www.rethinkprojectmanagement.com/assessment can help you identify the areas where AI integration can have the most significant impact.

NEXT STEPS TO ADOPT THE PMAI METHOD

Implementing the PMAI Method is a gradual process that requires careful planning and execution.

Here are some recommended next steps to begin your journey:

1. **Identify Suitable Projects:** Start by selecting one or two pilot projects where you can initially integrate the AI chatbot. Manageable, low-risk projects are ideal for this initial phase, allowing you to observe the chatbot's performance and refine your processes.

2. **Evaluate and Select an AI Chatbot:** Research and evaluate different text-based generative AI chatbots that cater to project management needs. Consider factors such as functionality, ease of integration, scalability, and overall cost.

3. **Develop a PMAI Implementation Plan:** Create a detailed plan outlining how you will incorporate the AI chatbot into each stage of the project management lifecycle, following the PMAI Method's 10 components. This plan should include specific use cases, roles and responsibilities, and success metrics.

4. **Train Your Team:** Provide comprehensive training to your project management team on using the selected AI chatbot effectively. Encourage them to experiment and explore the chatbot's capabilities, fostering a culture of continuous learning and adaptation.

5. **Establish Governance and Guidelines:** Develop clear guidelines and governance structures to ensure the responsible and ethical use of the AI chatbot. Address issues such as data privacy, decision accountability, and potential biases.

6. **Pilot and Iterate:** Implement the PMAI Method on your selected pilot projects, closely monitoring performance and gathering feedback from stakeholders. Use this experience to refine your processes, identify areas for improvement, and prepare for broader adoption.

7. **Expand and Scale:** Once you've achieved initial success and buy-in, gradually expand the use of the PMAI Method to more projects and teams within your organization. Continuously refine and optimize your processes as adoption grows.

BECOMING A PIONEER IN AI-DRIVEN PROJECT MANAGEMENT

By embracing the PMAI Method and integrating text-based generative AI chatbots into your project management workflows, you have the opportunity to become a pioneer in this emerging field. As an early adopter, you'll gain a competitive advantage, positioning yourself and your organization at the forefront of innovation.

To truly establish yourself as a thought leader in AI-driven project management, consider the following steps:

1. **Share Your Experiences:** Document your journey with the PMAI Method, capturing successes, challenges, and lessons learned. Share these insights through blog posts,

webinars, or industry events, contributing to the growing body of knowledge in this area.

2. **Participate in Professional Communities:** Join relevant professional associations, online forums, and networking groups focused on project management and AI integration. Engage in discussions, share best practices, and learn from others who are on similar paths.

3. **Seek Out Opportunities for Collaboration:** Collaborate with researchers, academics, or industry experts who specialize in AI and project management. These partnerships can lead to innovative solutions, joint publications, or speaking engagements, further solidifying your expertise.

4. **Continuous Learning and Development:** Stay up-to-date with the latest advancements in AI technology, project management methodologies, and industry trends. Pursue relevant certifications, attend conferences, and continuously refine your skills to maintain your competitive edge.

5. **Mentor and Inspire Others:** As you gain experience and expertise, consider mentoring others who are interested in implementing the PMAI Method. Share your knowledge, provide guidance, and inspire the next generation of AI-driven project managers.

By taking these steps, you'll not only position yourself as a pioneer but also contribute to the advancement of the project management profession as a whole.

EMBRACING THE FUTURE WITH THE PMAI METHOD

The future of project management lies in the seamless integration of cutting-edge technologies like AI. By implementing the PMAI Method, you'll be at the forefront of this revolution, optimizing your processes, enhancing productivity, and delivering unprecedented project success.

Don't let doubts or hesitations hold you back. Engage with text-based generative AI chatbots, develop a strategic implementation plan, and embrace a mindset of continuous learning and innovation. The PMAI Method provides a roadmap to navigate the challenges of the present while achieving the desired outcomes and "prizes" that define success in the IT project management realm.

Take action today by emailing me at [email address] to discuss how you can begin your journey with the PMAI Method. Alternatively, attend one of my upcoming workshops or complete the PMAI Readiness Assessment to evaluate your organization's preparedness for AI integration.

The future is here, and it's driven by the fusion of human expertise and artificial intelligence. Unlock your full potential as a project manager by becoming a pioneer in this exciting new frontier. The PMAI Method awaits – embrace it and witness the transformative impact it can have on your projects, your career, and your industry.

Ready to take the first step towards implementing the PMAI Method? Start by engaging with our ProjectPal GPT. Visit: www.rethinkprojectmanagement.com

CONCLUSIONS: THE FUTURE IS AI

As we stand on the precipice of an unprecedented technological revolution, the integration of text-based generative AI chatbots into project management is poised to reshape the landscape forever. This transformative journey has the potential to elevate project managers to new heights of efficiency, effectiveness, and strategic impact within their organizations.

Throughout this exploration, we have delved into the present-day challenges faced by project managers in the IT industry. Rapid technological advancements, increased project complexity, the shift to remote work environments, and stringent cybersecurity requirements have created a demanding and ever-evolving terrain. Navigating these obstacles while striving for successful project delivery, stakeholder satisfaction, and personal growth can be a daunting task.

However, the advent of text-based generative AI chatbots presents a powerful ally in this endeavor. By harnessing the capabilities of these intelligent assistants, project managers can streamline their workflows, enhance communication, mitigate risks, and optimize resource allocation – all while fostering a culture of continuous learning and improvement.

Imagine a world where a virtual assistant is at your side, ready to tackle the most intricate project details with precision and efficiency. From breaking down complex requirements into actionable plans to distilling lengthy documents into concise insights, the chatbot becomes an indispensable tool for project initiation and preparation.

As projects unfold, the chatbot's role expands, offering a range of invaluable functionalities. Meeting summaries are automatically generated, ensuring that key decisions and action items are never lost in the chaos of daily operations. Meanwhile, potential risks are proactively identified, and mitigation strategies are proposed, empowering project managers to stay ahead of potential roadblocks.

The chatbot's capabilities extend beyond mere task management; it becomes a facilitator of team collaboration and communication. Tasks are delegated seamlessly, progress is tracked in real-time, and timely reminders keep everyone aligned and focused on project milestones. Comprehensive status reports are generated effortlessly, providing stakeholders with transparent and up-to-date information, fostering trust and ensuring project success.

Moreover, the chatbot serves as a dynamic repository of best practices, lessons learned, and organizational standards. This centralized knowledge base promotes continuous learning, enabling project managers and their teams to consistently improve and adapt to emerging trends and methodologies.

But the benefits of text-based generative AI chatbots extend far beyond the boundaries of individual projects. By optimizing resource allocation based on project requirements and constraints, organizations can maximize efficiency and reduce waste. Furthermore, the chatbot's training and onboarding capabilities empower teams with the necessary skills and knowledge, fostering a culture of professional development and growth.

As we envision the future of project management with text-based generative AI chatbots, the possibilities are truly boundless. These intelligent assistants will become integral partners, augmenting human intelligence and capabilities, enabling project managers to focus on strategic decision-making, innovation, and driving transformative change within their organizations.

Imagine a world where project proposals, presentations, and other content are generated with the assistance of the chatbot, freeing up time for critical thinking and creative problem-solving. Envision a future where project managers can seamlessly navigate the complexities of digital transformation initiatives, leveraging the chatbot's insights and recommendations to ensure successful outcomes.

Furthermore, as the technology continues to evolve, the integration of text-based generative AI chatbots will undoubtedly expand into new domains. Natural language processing capabilities will enable more intuitive and conversational interactions, fostering a deeper symbiosis between human project managers and their AI assistants. Advancements in machine learning and data analysis will further enhance the chatbot's ability to identify patterns, anticipate trends, and provide increasingly sophisticated recommendations.

As we embrace this future, it is crucial to acknowledge the ethical considerations and responsible implementation of AI technologies. Ensuring data privacy, algorithmic fairness, and transparency will be paramount to building trust and fostering widespread adoption of these powerful tools.

Additionally, the human element of project management will

remain indispensable. While text-based generative AI chatbots will augment and enhance decision-making processes, they will not replace the essential leadership, emotional intelligence, and creative problem-solving skills that human project managers possess.

The journey towards this future is not without challenges, but the rewards are immense. By embracing the power of text-based generative AI chatbots, project managers can unlock unprecedented levels of productivity, efficiency, and strategic impact. They will be empowered to navigate the complexities of the modern IT landscape with confidence, delivering projects that exceed stakeholder expectations and drive organizational success.

In this era of rapid change and digital transformation, those who embrace the potential of text-based generative AI chatbots will be at the forefront of innovation, leading their teams and organizations towards a future defined by excellence, agility, and continuous growth.

As we stand at the cusp of this revolution, the choice is clear: project managers can either resist the tide of change or ride the wave of technological advancement, leveraging the power of text-based generative AI chatbots to elevate their craft and shape the future of project management.

The future is not a distant possibility; it is an imminent reality, and those who adapt and embrace the transformative potential of text-based generative AI chatbots will be the architects of this new era, leaving an indelible mark on the industry and paving the way for generations to come.

NEXT STEPS

Now that you understand the transformative potential of generative AI for project management, it's time to take action.

A great first step is to complete the AI Project Manager Readiness Assessment. This free online tool evaluates your current practices and pinpoints areas where an AI assistant could enhance efficiency, collaboration, risk management, and more.

Upon completing the assessment, you'll receive a personalized report with your readiness score and tailored recommendations. The report also highlights how ReThink Project Management's ProjectPal, a cutting-edge generative AI chatbot, could revolutionize your project approach.

ProjectPal is designed to be your dedicated AI companion throughout the entire project lifecycle. With natural language interaction, ProjectPal can assist with tasks like:

- Drafting plans, reports, and other documents.
- Analyzing data to identify risks and optimize schedules.
- Automating routine updates and stakeholder communication.
- Providing on-demand expertise and best practice

recommendations.

To find out more, visit www.rethinkprojectmanagement.com

Don't miss this opportunity to future-proof your project management skills. Get started today by taking the free assessment at www.rethinkprojectmanagement.com/assessment

Let ProjectPal streamline your processes so you can focus on strategic leadership and driving successful project outcomes.

ABOUT THE AUTHOR

DR. SHELDON ST. CLAIR

Dr. Sheldon St. Clair is a highly accomplished project management professional with extensive experience leading successful projects and programs across various industries. As a PMO leader and consultant, he has leveraged his broad skillset and certifications to drive organizational success through effective planning, financial management, and resource optimization.

With a strong educational foundation, including a Ph.D. in project management, an MBA in finance, and a BSc (Hons) in mathematics and computing, Sheldon has cultivated a deep understanding of the intricate dynamics involved in managing complex projects. His expertise spans multiple disciplines, allowing him to navigate diverse challenges with ease.

Throughout his career, Sheldon has amassed a wealth of experience in various industries, including construction, banking, and finance. One of his notable achievements was managing the intricate ICB Ring-Fence banking reform project, an undertaking that required meticulous planning and execution. Additionally, he has successfully established and operated multiple PMO environments, showcasing his ability to build and lead high-performing teams.

Sheldon's commitment to excellence has been recognized by his peers, as evidenced by his role as a judge for the prestigious PMO Global Alliance Awards Competition in 2019 and 2020. This honor highlights his reputation as a thought leader in the field of project management.

Moreover, Sheldon is a firm believer in the power of emerging technologies to revolutionize project management practices. He has actively pursued certifications in areas like Generative AI and has become adept at leveraging cutting-edge tools, such as GPT models, to enhance project management processes and drive business success.

With a passion for solving real-world project management problems through innovation, Sheldon has contributed his expertise through several acclaimed publications, including "Project Management for the Modern Professional: Strategies, Techniques, and Insights", "Setting Up Your PMO: A Guide for Managers and Consultants", "Your Project Management Questions Answered: The 25 Things Project Managers Most Want to Know", and "Smarter, Faster, Better: Project Management Templates."

Sheldon's unique blend of academic excellence, hands-on experience, and a forward-thinking approach to technology has positioned him as a respected authority in the field of project management. His commitment to continuous learning and his ability to adapt to emerging trends make him an invaluable asset to organizations seeking to optimize their project management capabilities and achieve sustainable success.

Printed in Great Britain
by Amazon

42017902R00076